MY BEST THINKING

The Highs and Lows of Rehab

Sarina Wheatman

Michael Terence
Publishing

First published in paperback by
Michael Terence Publishing in 2020
www.mtp.agency

Copyright © 2020 Sarina Wheatman

Sarina Wheatman has asserted the right to be identified as the
author of this work in accordance with the
Copyright, Designs and Patents Act 1988

ISBN 9781913289782

No part of this publication may be reproduced, stored in a retrieval
system, or transmitted, in any form or by any means, electronic,
mechanical, photocopying, recording or otherwise, without the prior
permission of the publishers

Cover image
Copyright © Iriana88w, Penchan Pumila

Cover design
Copyright © 2020 Michael Terence Publishing

Contents

Introduction i

1: Hangovers, Blackouts and Shame 1

2: The Fog and Confusion Lifts 7

3: Pieces of the Puzzle Start to Fit 17

4: Megan, Her Pets, and Pavla 41

5: 'I'll Do It Tomorrow' Becomes Obsolete 55

6: Rules, Regulations and Taming the Rebels 64

7: Aiden, His Lost Digits, and Pete 76

8: Hamish and Running from the Law 83

9: Comings and Goings and Brendon's Deception ... 94

10: The New Gang in Town 105

11: Bloody Meetings and Megan's story 111

12: Aftercare Meeting at Moriatta Falls/Relapse 121

13: Pretty Names, Ugly Behaviours 129

14: Megan, Aiden and the Great Escape 138

15: Vanda the Girl in Flight 147

16: Characteristics of a Functional Family 153

17: Rick's Unhealthy Game 159

18: The Invisible Child Made Visible 166

19: Endings, New Beginnings - Repeat 171

Resources 185

Introduction

This is a fictional story about Rehab and some brave people's bid for freedom from addiction. If that sounds dramatic or the stories that are told within the book seem far-fetched, I can assure you, they are anything but. This is a work of fiction. Any resemblance to actual events or people, living or dead, is entirely coincidental. After all, as one of the characters in the book says, 'confidentiality is a cornerstone of the recovery world'. It wouldn't be the right thing to do to tell, without filter, the struggles real live people have in their bid for freedom. However the people and the stories depict the mad thinking that always accompanies the disease of addiction.

I have worked in the Recovery world for over 30 years, so have witnessed many versions of the things I talk about in the book. Of course with every story about recovery there is also a story about a descent into the hell that is untreated addiction. I was one of those unfortunates whose life was spiralling out of control, but I managed to find recovery and significantly have managed to hold onto it. I began to write about the world of addiction first of all in non-fiction books as a way of changing perceptions about the disease. It is my firm belief that if the world can change its ideas about addiction, about what it is and how to treat it, then perhaps the devastating deaths by addiction, or the catastrophic relapse rates could be improved. My non-fiction books about Addiction and Recovery did not set our world on fire, so I hoped a fictionalised story about 'hell and redemption' might encourage more people to read and find out about addiction and recovery. I am therefore including in this story lots of references to helping agencies, support systems and organizations that exist to aid and support people with this perplexing, maddening, insane illness.

I have worked as an Addiction Therapist in England, Jersey and Holland. I hold an accreditation with The Federation of Drug and Alcohol Professionals (FDAP), as well as a little cache of accreditations that I have collected over the years. Also for many years I have involved myself in research and on-going training about this disease. I have always worked in Rehabs, always using the same methods in treatment as I use in my own life. As well as writing books about the subject of addiction and recovery I also have a small private practice.

I have enjoyed many years of Recovery and have immense gratitude for my great fortune in finding a treatment method that works for me. I am also hugely grateful to the men and woman who have helped me first of all to find recovery, and then of course to keep it.

Recovery is certainly a beautiful thing, but I never forget that in order for recovery to happen there will be a story of a relentless progressive illness that each person will have lived through. I am constantly amazed by how little the general public know or understand about addiction. I am always shocked when the reputation, that addicts are selfish, weak-willed people who lack morals is shouted about in the media. I have wanted to change this perception for many years.

My books are an extension of my work in rehabs where I attempt to educate, inform and treat this baffling disease. There is still argument about if it's an illness or not. Treatment is still a kind of lottery system. Lucky if you find something that works for you, lucky when the system you choose tells you that Abstinence is the key to everything, and that the real problem is the way you think! 'My best Thinking', the title of this book attempts to illustrate how absolutely crazy the thinking of practicing addicts is. It is also the only illness where denial is so great that the addict will go to great lengths to conceal the truth from self and others. It is time this Mental Health Illness got rebranded, maybe then people who have it will find help quicker, or our young, the next generation can be taught how to avoid falling into its trap.

The inclusion about suicide awareness and Moriatta Falls as the name of the Rehab, have been created to honour the memory of the daughter of one of my oldest friends, Lou Gannon. Lou's daughter Darcie sadly did not survive her journey into the hell of untreated addiction and other mental health problems. Lou, has allowed me to talk openly about some of the things she and her daughter went through. Darcie was much loved and always sadly missed. She remains an inspiration to me to be part of the change in the ideas about Addiction. Statistics about suicide, talk about 80% of successful suicides have alcohol or other drugs in the mix.

'Changing perceptions one book at a time', has been my motto ever since I put pen to paper, it remains my drive and ambition. I have attempted to introduce the reader to a birds-eye view of what happens in a rehab. Many more things occur of course, but it is my hope that people seeking help will discover there is nothing more frightening than untreated addiction, Admission to rehab is relatively easy in comparison. I sincerely hope that someone, anyone, everyone will pick up this book, find the information they need and in turn find Recovery. The 'patients and stories' are fiction, the 'workshops, lectures and information' pages which are written in **BOLD** are all non-fiction.

1: Hangovers, Blackouts and Shame

"OMG, what is that thumping in my head?" I whispered to myself, "where am I?"

Gingerly I open my eyes, and immediately wished I had not. The room was spinning, I'm dizzy and sick to my stomach my heart thumping in tandem with my throbbing head.

At least I have a heartbeat I thought, I'm alive then. Which was a strange comfort as so often lately I have, especially at moments like this, not wanted to live.

Nausea and pain, where am I? I wish I was dead; Oh God I'm going to be sick; I search desperately for a bathroom and make it in time. I retch and retch until all my shuddering body can produce is bile. My head hurts, my eyes streaming, bile and vomit mingling. I can smell the alcohol and other vile odours on my body. I desperately try to keep my hair out of the toilet bowl.

In the midst of this undignified ritual, the door to my room opens.

My room? I thought, who's room, which room? I have no idea what room or where. Where the hell am I?

The figure in the doorway stands in shadow, I try to blink away the tears and flush away the vomit, I am kneeling by the toilet. I am in pain, I know this feeling well, another hangover, another few days to get back to fighting fit, another several days to piece together my latest shameful behaviours. "Who are you?" I boldly say, although my voice is a little more tremulous than I would have liked. I hide my shaking hands the best way I can, but I'm stuck on this bathroom floor. Thankfully the retching has stopped but everything else is painful. The room is dark and warm, but my eyes hurt and I'm freezing cold and shivering like crazy.

"Hi Mimi, my name is Juliette, do you know where you are?" Juliette continues to talk without waiting for an answer, which I cannot give anyway. It is all I can do to raise my head and try to stand.

Juliette says she is a nurse. "Let me help you," as she takes my arm, and with a cloth rinses away the vomit from my face and hair. "Looks like you have a nasty case of alcohol poisoning." She is gentle but firm as she wipes. "We can't give you anything yet to help with the sickness, you have to read 100 or less on our breathalyser, we'll keep monitoring you until this happens."

Oh God No! I told them I wouldn't do rehab, singing the Amy Winehouse's song in my mind, I don't want to, I will not do it. Why the fuck should I? I'm not hurting anyone, it's my body I can do what I like with it. This familiar refrain plays out in my head as Nurse Juliette helps me up and leads me to a bed. As soon as she said 'Nurse', I know immediately where I am, this had been threatened to me so many times by various people, I had threatened me for heaven's sake, when the trouble mounted, and the sickness was bad. I knew I could not go on doing this indefinitely. But not yet…Oh God what's going on? As I sank into bed I prayed for release, and mercifully it came as I passed out and slept away the next few hours.

The next time I opened my eyes, thankfully much of the pain in my head had stopped hurting, the nausea had almost gone, and I could open my eyes without wanting to faint. Now all that was left was that fragile feeling in my whole body as it tries to heal from the latest assault by toxins and poisons, a blank mind about what had happened and a huge fear building in me about what might happen next. I had a massive black bruise down one side of my arm, and a graze on my cheek. Everything hurt and it looked like I'd been in a fight or accident of some sort. As these thoughts flashed through my mind, my heart nearly stopped when I thought about my car and driving here.

Oh no! was all I could think.

"Ah! you are awake," says the figure standing in the doorway to my room, "do you remember me?"

"Hi Juliette, yeah I remember you were decent to me when I was throwing up. That's about it though I don't remember how I got here, or where here is."

I had arrived in the early hours, driven my car on my own,

shit, 60 miles in blackout! Now in the cold light of day I have no recollection of the journey, the route I took or arriving. How is that possible? I thought, but a creeping feeling of dread was starting to crawl all over me. Driving in blackout, bruises? Please, please no, I silently prayed.

"Your car was in the carpark," Juliette said, "parked diagonally across the courtyard! Don't worry we've sorted it out," she said, "you gave us your keys no problem when you arrived. Which is a bit of a blessing as so many people refuse to give up this bit of independence, and we sometimes have huge problems taking them from you. Running away again is one of the problems in the early days of being here."

"Can I go out to the car?" I asked, "I need to get something from the glovebox."

"We will need to accompany you, I'm afraid some patients try to smuggle all sorts of things into the building, and the car is the easiest way to do it. Get dressed first though and then we will find someone to go with you."

I had been talking about coming to rehab for ages, made lots of tentative phone calls asking price and directions and how long I needed to stay. Apparently in my last blackout, I had actually made the decision all by myself and checked in. No-one to blame but me! That's two mistakes I think, checking in and handing in the keys. And now given the state of my body I was frightened I might have hit someone on my way here. I have to go check that car.

"Don't look so worried my dear, memory blanks happen more often than you would think," said Juliette, "people arrive here in lots of ways, either by their own hand or by the desperate measures of family or friends. But don't worry about that yet, I'm here to take some more stats, the doctor will come and see you and then we can start your detox so you can start to feel a little better." With that, I had my blood pressure taken and was breathalysed, must have passed the test because I am given some medication to help with the symptoms. Diazepam they said, to help with the detoxification. Doctors and nurses leave me alone after taking some blood, and I am given instructions to get up and dress. Sure enough within a short space of time I began to feel a little more human, less fragile, less tetchy. I get into the shower; it is lovely relief standing under the healing cleansing water. Then as I put on clean clothes I thanked whatever gods there were for small mercies, I had my clothes packed for ages, knowing I would come here someday. Kept the case stashed in the car just in case. The thought of the car loomed darkly in my head, I still couldn't remember anything about an accident as I began to try to piece together the events of the last hours and days, leading up to my admission to bloody rehab. I don't want to remember to be honest, I know it will be shameful, I know I will bitterly regret everything I said and did. I know I don't want to know but I also know that I have to in order to figure out what to do next.

The door opens again. A head peers around the door.

"Bloody hell!" her words softened somewhat with a sympathetic smile, "you look rough, I'm Rita, I'm going to show you around if you are able. Don't look so scared I'm not staff I'm just like you, a patient, but just a few days further on."

Rita appeared a little bit older than me, she looked and smelled fabulous, makeup, nice clothes, short spiky hair. Hard to imagine she was a patient. She was chatting on about having been here for 3 weeks and how amazing everything was. I wanted her to shut up to be honest, my head was hurting again, but held my tongue and just listened. Not sure it was nice to be in the company of someone so happy and fragrant whilst I felt and, as her initial exclamation told me, looked vile. But I needed to find out what and where etc, I needed to figure out the lie of the land and how to get out of this place, perhaps this was the best way to do it. I was still feeling very fragile and disorientated, maybe some fresh air and company would help I thought. She led me out of my room. Room 12 it said on the door.

Of course I am able, I thought as I took some deep breaths and shoved my shaking hands in my pockets. I put the problem of checking my car to one side for now, after all I thought, the nurse said they had parked it properly, surely they would have said if anything was amiss?

2: The Fog and Confusion Lifts

Rita and I start this little tour, me gingerly and slow, so's not to jar my aching limbs, and she with enthusiasm. Kindly slowing to my pace as we walk around the building and grounds. She tells me there are six other residents in the place.

Only six? That doesn't sound like many, not so popular then I think. She tells me it is an exclusive and small rehab on the South Coast. With what is known as a rolling programme,

"What the hell is that?" I say.

"It just means that patients come and go and join and leave the group depending on the length of their stay. So sometimes there can be six people here at a time, and sometimes more or sometimes less. There is a maximum number of twelve residents. The treatment centre is hidden away in a private woodland. Lots of well-known people have been here," Rita says, "even though you would never know it is so private," she rambles on, me not telling her I already know some of this stuff. Secretly pleased to be hearing I can be anonymous; no-one will know I'm here unless I tell them.

"Can we smoke here?"

I am desperate for some nicotine to take away some of the vile taste in my mouth. Rita leads me to the smoking area; "We are lucky," she says, "most places have banned smoking, but the staff here have made it possible for us to smoke in designated areas."

The smoking area is really a dismal place, smelly and cold out in the grounds, ashtrays and butts, but at least we can satisfy those nicotine urges. Someone has hung a windchime to try to pretty up this place. It doesn't work.

"We try to keep it tidy but, well a fag is a fag, isn't it?" This disembodied voice comes rolling round us from the smoking area, the voice sounds Australian.

A fag is a fag, I think as I join two other people who are puffing away looking at me with what I can honestly say is suspicion.

Rita introduces me to Brendon, who is indeed Australian, and Aiden whose accent I have not yet worked out; I nod and sit down and accept the light that Brendon offers to my unlit cigarette.

"Hi," they say in unison. Aiden holds out his hand to shake mine. "How're you doing?" he adds.

Oh God a ponytail, I think, but I smile, and say "pretty shit actually, just got here."

"Yeah we know, detox is the worst bit. Don't give up, take it slow. Promise you will be ok in a few days."

Rita stays out of this circle of smoke, "I don't," she says, "but you carry on."

Brendon says, "I got here two weeks ago and feel so much better. Detox is the worst of times, but it passes quickly, the Diazepam they give you is a marvel, just do what the Docs tell you and you will soon be smiling again. Epic parking Blue, nasty dent in the bumper," says Brendon in his best Australian drawl.

My heart nearly stops again, and I can hardly get my breath. Trying desperately to change the subject I ask what goes on all day in a place like this. The car will have to wait.

"Well, there's group, and the programme and meeting lots of people who used to do what we do but are now clean," says Brendon, "it's scary but actually it will all make sense in a while. They say this is the best rehab on the South Coast."

"Where exactly on the South Coast?" I ask as I greedily inhale the nicotine curling around my face. Plotting my escape, needing to find out where and what and how.

I have of course, admitted myself to 'Moriatta Falls' named by a talented and very beautiful person who had survived her own suicide attempt at this famed location, and opened up her own rehab because of it. Her survival and story is written into the advertising material for Moriatta Falls, which Rita and Brendon now recite to me.

Moriatta Falls

Moriatta Falls is a clinic for addictions, founded in 2001 by Margot Laird. Margot's vision for her treatment centre was for it to be exclusive, elegant but accessible. She made sure for instance that her charitable trust were always able to provide a place for people who were in financial difficulties. Her vision began after surviving years of untreated addiction herself, which culminated in a plan she had made to take her own life. She tells a tale of a miraculous turnaround in her thinking which began when she was told that she was suffering from untreated addiction. She had believed that she was mad, that her depression and anxiety which were ferocious were the only culprits in her worsening mood and behaviours. To be told that her use of alcohol and prescription medication **as well** as the other diagnosis were the reason for her out of control behaviour was shocking, but life-changing. She went into treatment, got well, and decided that she could make a difference in the world. She called her rehab Moriatta Falls to be ever reminded that out of control addiction is deadly. She describes how she had been looking up online, places and ways to kill herself, only one day before finding the doctor that gave her the right diagnosis. Margot wrote a poem about the place she had found online to honour all those who had not been as lucky as she had been in avoiding this ultimate expression of self-harm. She wanted it to be a reminder of how close to taking her own life she had come. She had been travelling Australia in her youth, the freedom she experienced hastened her addictive tendencies, so it became the place she was the sickest, but also the place she had found recovery. The name was symbolic of the risks all addicts take when living with untreated addiction. She wanted to create a living memorial to all those who had been or will be unable to find their way out of that maze of twisted sick thinking that is created in addiction.

Moriatta Falls

She chose this place from thousands she
Had access to.
It was said she googled it
Made it real,
And went to see,
She chose this place because
Maybe like me, she thought it
Sounded beautiful.
It sounded peaceful, or even spectacular –
So she went to see,
Thought it fit –
Didn't think –
Held her breath and jumped.

"Ghoulish of course," says Aiden who chimes into this piece of the conversation. "Ghoulish and sick, but pretty effective none-the-less. Margot goes around the world talking about suicide awareness and addiction."

"Do you think addiction is deadly?" I ask. "Do you think it's an illness? Can people recover?"

"I have my own ghoulish story," said Aiden. As he holds up his left hand and I notice he has lost two of his fingers. He smiles wryly and says, "it makes holding things a little bit difficult."

"What happened to your hand?" It is black and blue with very obvious gaps where fingers should be.

"Hummmm tell you later when I know you better," says Aiden," but for now let's just say it is a result of out of control addiction."

I am shocked, at the casual way Aiden has said all of this and at the twinkle in his eyes when he talks about knowing me better. You must be bloody joking I think to myself.

"Yes addiction is an illness and it is deadly," says Brendon finishing off the conversation. "You will learn a lot in a place like this if you stick around. And if you stick around you just might recover. I don't know the real Moriatta falls, just in case you are wondering, Oz is a big place, but I do know it is a place a lot of jumpers have used as their last goodbye, very pretty by all accounts."

"OK boys, leave her alone, she's just got here, I am just

showing Mimi around, time enough for the lectures and the lessons. Be nice!"

"Sorry Mimi, no offence meant."

Sorry, no offence meant, one of my favourite sayings after all, having had to use it many times, in many different situations, the latest in the hours just before the dreaded blackout struck and I remember nothing about the kamikaze drive here.

Blackout

The evening has started like many others, getting dressed up, and that lovely excitement at the pit of the stomach, who will be there, who will I meet? Maybe tonight JT will be around, and we can finally get this relationship back on track. I was out with the gang at one of our usual haunts, the alcohol was flowing, the music was epic, and I was on top form. Laughing and dancing, flirting up a storm with all and sundry. There was nothing in my flirts, anyone who knew me would tell you that, I reserved all my seriousness for JT but of course this was only known to my tribe, strangers did not know I was only having fun waiting for my main man to arrive.

The problem that night, started when I was pushed roughly by a woman who was twice my size, leave him alone she hissed at me. All the fun immediately left the room and only the hiss and the angry woman were visible to me. Me, never a fighter, backed down immediately and took refuge in the women's toilets. She followed me in unfortunately, but ever the diplomat, I managed to convince her I meant no harm and eventually she left me alone. I slunk back to the bar; the adrenalin hit that the interaction with the 'She Bear' had given me, coursed through my veins. Knowing better, but not caring after the fright I had, set about ordering more drinks, forgetting about her, and JT and anything else that troubled me.

The next thing I became aware of was my curled-up body lying on the bottom of some bunk beds. A stranger was leaning over me with a damp cloth trying to get my attention.

Wake up Mimi please, wake up we are about to sail. I peer up at the man standing over me, dressed in a uniform.

Seeing his face close to mine, I immediately came to and realised by the thrum of the floor and surroundings that I was on a vessel, I could hear a Tannoy in the distance and realised with alarm that the thrum was the sound of engines, the disembodied voice on the Tannoy was telling me we were about to set sail.

At least he's a captain, I remember thinking. Snobbish and ridiculous even in this crazy predicament.

Oh God, get me off this thing now. We hurried to the side of the ship and the gangway, and with barely time to spare was able to say farewell and disembark. Johann the man I had chatted up at the bar and who had been trying to wake me, stroked my face in goodbye and said, you really should not drink so much, I handed him my visitors badge and walked down the gangway. Shamed yet again by my antics and somewhat saddened by Johann's kind gesture in stroking my face.

My blackouts were becoming more problematic, fine one minute and waking up on a ship the next. I had simply no recollection of anything that had happened in-between. I thought Johann had seemed a gentleman, so was fairly certain he would have acted appropriately with me, but how many more times was I going to chance my luck. I shivered as I thought about what could have happened.

I watched the ship set sail, made my way back to the bar and found the friends I had started the evening with. I had been gone for only an hour, and not really missed, the room was busy and loud with excited chat, I told no-one what had just occurred. My shame at yet another escapade was pushed away in the next drink, and the next and the next, and then my next 'come to' was in Moriatta Falls rehab. I had no idea where my friends were, or if I had eventually met up with JT, just a big frightening blank where a memory should be.

Shit, didn't mean to cause offence, but this whole story was offensive. Maybe I should stay and try to work out why I continued to act like a little savage and ruin everything I touched. Maybe they were right I was sick, and my behaviour was part of an illness. Lord knows I need to change. Although I did not know it yet, that one sentence was the beginning of my salvation, right here right now albeit not knowing how or even wanting to change, the seeds of change were planted. A blackout, a shameful story, a hangover and a realisation was all it took. As well as the last fifteen years of increasingly mad stories of a similar ilk.

I was to learn that everyone here at the clinic had shameful pieces of a puzzle we had to find and fit together. Even Brendon who had sounded so callous and uncaring, talking about suicide in such a matter of fact way. Even Mr Super confident Aiden had pieces of this puzzle which were sad and shameful, ugly or funny. All of us had this in common. But the scarier thought was, they had said we all had to talk about this stuff. OUT LOUD!

"Don't look so scared," said Rita kindly, "nobody ends up in rehab because life is hunky-dory, all of us have some sort of crisis ticking away there in the background, which has to be found, exposed and worked through if we are ever to be able to move on. The things that happen to us are not the reason we end up as addicts, but they certainly contribute to the overall picture. If we don't start talking, nothing can change."

3: Pieces of the Puzzle Start to Fit

After my smoke in the garden with the boys and Rita, she accompanies me to other parts of the establishment, showed me the dining room, the patients' lounge. All the while giving me a running commentary on her life as well as snippets about others in the clinic. She was a font of information. I called her 'The Oracle' it appeared she knew everything.

Other Patients

Rita, 46 years old, married with 2 children, Rita said she had been a stay at home mum for a few years. She and her husband had made a lot of money in the music business. Before she left the business to concentrate on their daughters, life had been sweet. She didn't know when exactly but somewhere in the lifestyle they now had, they grew apart. Her husband was always away on business, and she suspected he was having an affair. She said in order to cope with his 'secret' life, her drinking which had always been manageable somehow grew unmanageable, she had begun to make trips to the doctor with her depression and inability to sleep, until she realised she was taking multiple amounts of prescription pills washed down with lots of alcohol. Her hazy days became interspersed with hazy shopping trips, lunches 'with the girls' became crying fests, until no more invitations came. Her loneliness and unhappiness she said almost took her to that 'dark place'. Rita said that the worst part of her story was that whilst her husband was away on yet another business trip her daughters who were 16 and 17, had staged what is routinely called an intervention. She explained her daughters had confronted her one day and told her she had to go to rehab. They had found out that there were such things as 'interventionists' and had been coached in the right things to say and do. They couldn't stand living with her this way anymore. If she didn't go they would leave home. They had done some research about rehabs with the help of the therapist working with them and had decided that Moriatta Falls looked the best. Rita added this place, and their bravery in confronting her had saved her life. However she was having a real hard time forgiving herself, she was so ashamed that her precious daughters had to act like this. - Alcohol and Prescription Pills – Dual Diagnosis of Depression and Insomnia.

Rita ended her story by saying breezily, my claim to fame is ending up just like Margot Laird taking the same poisons as she did and wanting to die like she did. She said all of this with not an iota of self-pity, just facts, brutal and sad.

Brendon – 40 years old, Rita said that Brendon was indeed an Australian, real funny and kind when you got to know him. He'd been in England for ages, and in this rehab for two weeks. She said he would tell me the rest of his story when I joined group. – Ecstasy Cocaine, Alcohol.

Aiden – 29 years old, always flirting, but had a girlfriend. Aiden came from somewhere 'up North', been here for a little less time than Brendon, but they appeared best buddies. Aiden was a chef and traveller. Rita said the missing fingers were still a mystery, no doubt we would learn what happened soon. Watch him he thinks he's God's Gift. – Cannabis – Cocaine – Anything – Dual Diagnosis of Bi-Polar.

"Ah ha!" I said, "I thought that twinkle in his eyes was a flirt! What's Bi-Polar?"

"Yes, stay clear lovie," said Rita, "nothing good will come from hooking up with anyone in here. Not too sure of all the details of Bi-Polar, but let's just say Aiden has massive mood swings. He'll tell you himself that the meds he is on now are a lifesaver."

Pavla – 42-year-old ex-model and socialite, turned shop owner. Pavla was lovely, a little ditzy at times, but lovely none-the-less. You will love her accent. Been in treatment for several days, she will be telling her story tomorrow. – Alcohol, Amphetamines, maybe an Eating Disorder – Dual Diagnosis of Depression.

Hamish – 67-year-old teacher retired, married with 4 adult children. Hamish is a real old-fashioned gent. Turns his nose up a bit at some of the language and fun and games some of the group get up to. He's been here a week I think says Rita, he's still a bit jittery in his detox. Keeps himself to himself. So I'm not too sure really what his story is all about. I expect he'll be asked to tell it soon. – Alcohol and Workaholism.

Megan – 19-year-old student, Megan was the baby of the group, but super smart and knows all about every drug under the sun, you will like her. She will tell you herself that she has one of the Bursary places that are available. Said her parents couldn't afford to send her here and keep her in University, so she's very grateful to Moriatta Falls. – Ketamine, Cannabis, Self harming.

Pete – 30-year-old marketing whizz-kid been at the clinic a few days and still really sick in detox, he hadn't made it to group yet – Cocaine, Speed, Alcohol and Dual diagnosis of Depression and Anxiety.

"No-one can came to group until the medics say they are able. Sometimes it takes days and days for someone to be ready health-wise, or as in your case you are up and about from the get-go."

Rita went onto say she couldn't say much else about the others as it was their stories to tell, I would meet everyone at mealtimes and in group. Group was the most important part of what was done in rehab she said, this is where people begin to be taken apart and then put together again.

"Sounds bloody horrible," I said.

"It is and it isn't," says Rita, "I won't tell you too much about what happens here, but don't be frightened, nothing is worse than continuing to live the way we did before we came here. The very fact you are here means you've recognised something was wrong and want to change." With that she gave me a little hug and left me at the door of number 12. My whirlwind tour and education about the rest of the 'guests' at Moriatta Falls had ended.

I arrived back to the sanctity of my room, already feeling it was my safe space. I arrived back feeling subdued and very thoughtful. I had to go and check my bloody car, but something in the things Rita had been saying had reached my addled brain and hurting heart. I was changing my mind about being here. Rita was right I did want to change, I did want something different for my life, I was so sick of the blackouts, the endless hangovers and being ill. But what the hell was group? I thought places like this did one to one counselling. I couldn't imagine how 'group' would help. To be quite honest thinking about 'group' almost made me pack my things and scarper again, but just as I was contemplating this, another knock, and Nurse Juliette put her head around the door and said I was due for some medication. With the lure of the calming tendrils of this drug in my head, I changed my mind one more time and followed the nurse to the Dispensary.

Staff at Moriatta Falls

Nurse Juliette, who I had met the day before led me to the place my medications were given out. She looked to be in her 50's, nice looking in a motherly kind of way. She said she had worked here since Margot Laird had opened the place. She said she was a Registered Mental Health Nurse (RMN for short) with many years of experience of working with addictions. She always added that this was her favourite rehab ever and felt honoured to work here.

Nurse Christophe was in the Dispensary giving out the medications to the patients. He was nice looking if a little avant-garde, he did not look like any nurse I had in my head, he was about 30 or 40, pretty stylish in weird sort of way, at least the style I could relate to and liked in a man. Not at all nurse like I thought, as he greeted me with a French accent.

I like you, I think, getting ready to bring my flirt on should it be needed. But I could see that this was not the time or the place, he was serious but kind and extremely busy. Plus the medication he was giving to each patient was the focal point of this interaction.

Nurse May looked interesting I thought, she was floating around between different rooms in the clinic, smiling and happy looking. Here was another one with an eccentric way of dressing, she favoured a boho kind of look. All flowing with exotic jewellery. On someone else this might look messy but Nurse May wore it well and exuded a comfortable kind of presence. She reminded me of festivals and Glastonbury. Rita said, May always had time for a kind word or two and had been at the clinic for several years.

"Everyone seems to have been here some time," I said to Rita who was waiting in the medication line with me," it must be an ok place to work, which in turn probably makes it an ok place for us? I'll reserve judgment on that though."

Rita just smiled and said it was best I made my own mind up about Moriatta Falls and the people who worked here.

She told me other Nurses I had yet to meet were **Ruby, Malc,** and **Alan.** I would meet them at different shifts, or at night during those witching hours when sleep will not come.

There were also Health Care Assistants, Housekeeping Staff, Chefs and Maintenance People. As well as all kind of administration people. They were a bit remote to most of us as they sat 'upstairs' in an office which we did not have access to.

A big busy place to look after I thought. A parallel universe almost, as this felt nothing like the outside world.

Rita said just before I received my meds," hang on, wait till I get mine and I'll accompany you to dinner."

"I don't really want to eat," I said, "I'm still feeling a bit sick."

"Well just come for 10 minutes to meet some of the others. It might make it easier to feel more at home here," said Rita.

All the patients that Rita had given me a quick roll call on were present at dinner except for Pete, still too sick to come to eat, said someone.

The conversation around the table turned to G.R.O.U.P.

"I must admit," I say, "I am a little freaked out at the thought of this thing called group, tell me about it, who runs it, how long do we have to do it, what happens?"

"We've got several therapists," says Brendon, "there is **Wolfie, (Wolfgang** really but everyone calls him Wolfie) Insists he is Wolfie and not Mr or anything formal. he seems to be the head honcho. He's a decent enough man, a little bit of a rottweiler to be honest but knows what he's doing in groups and always seems to hit the target with people. Great lectures. He is smart but we're all a smidge scared of him."

"What do you mean rottweiler and target?" My panic must have shown, because they all laughed and said, "don't worry, - it's for our own good," – and they laughed again.

"Don't worry," someone said, "we just mean he can be a bit fierce and detective-like, but whatever he's 'detecting' he always seems to hit the mark. He's ok really."

"We also work with a woman called **Sindy,** she's about 40ish says she is an addict, but can't see it myself," says Aiden, "she's too mainstream, but she's ok, in a barbie doll kind of way. Always hiding behind makeup, she's much too pretty for all that shit, but hey who am I to talk. Barbie/Sindy – see what I did there?" He says laughing. "Seriously though everyone needs a mask or two. Sindy knows her stuff and is generally pretty kind. When Wolfie is giving us a hard time, she will come in with a smile or kind word to make us feel better. She's got this insane eyebrow which when raised we all know to take notice, shut up or change direction."

"She sounds bloody awful," I say, "what's with the masks and eyebrows?"

"Nah, she's ok, you'll see when you start group," says Aiden.

I am also told about **Ellen** who's a student**,** and **Lorna** whose been counselling for about 5 years and several other people who drop in and out of group on a regular basis.

Enough difference in all of them so patients don't get bored, and lots of different talents from each of them. Sindy runs the family programme and does acupuncture too, which is brilliant to stop some of those vile detox symptoms. They want us to get off medications as quickly as possible, so their detoxes are pretty quick. Acupuncture swings in and is super helpful. There is also Yoga and a personal trainer. They are looking after our minds and bodies. We also go out walking once we get past detox stage When you get into the swing of it all, time goes quite fast. We have lots of different things we do each day, you won't be bored. With all this information buzzing round my head, I barely noticed the food, but my reluctance to eat it was noticed and I was told that the staff were pretty hot about nutrition and after tonight would have to have a good reason not to eat.

With everything this day had revealed and all the people I had met and had snippets of conversations with I felt absolutely washed out. I excused myself from the table, found my way to room 12 and went to bed. My whole body ached, I had another headache and for the life of me couldn't work out how to check the car or leave this bloody place.

Nightmares and Dreams

I had some disturbing dreams that night, quite mad and frightening, I was an Australian nurse working on a ship. I was playing poker in the casino and getting drunk with the captain. The other players all had Christophe's features and were in different stages of inebriation, all drinking Southern Comfort from bottles and singing Amy's song. The captain was having me thrown off his ship and swearing at me in French. The drive to an escape was dodgem like, I was swearing and screaming as I hit everything in sight. I awoke sweating and crying.

I went out to the nurse's station and found the nurses on duty.

"Don't worry," they said, "vivid dreams seem to be quite common at your stage of detox." Alan made me a cup of camomile tea and sat with me for some time as I calmed down and tried to go back to sleep.

"Best thing to do with these dreams is to write them down and talk about them in group. Some people even start a dream journal, it will be interesting to look back and be able to track your progress back to sanity. When you start dreaming like that it is stuff from the sub-conscious, things you might have forgotten or are trying to suppress that are working their way to the surface. It's quite normal to have using dreams or even nightmares, you just have to learn to take notice of them by talking about them and not just ignoring them. There are lots of books about the subject, and your dreams can actually teach you quite a bit about yourself, once you learn how to translate them of course, the language of dreams is not quite like everyday language."

I like the idea of dream journals, but this is not a normal dream, it's an omen and a nightmare and seemed to confirm my worst fears about hurting someone on my way to the clinic. I've got to check that bloody car.

More Staff

Alan, like the oracle, then begins to give me a little run down of himself and some of the other staff I had yet to meet. He said he'd been at the clinic for several years and loved the place. He said he had, in another lifetime been working as a nurse in another hospital. His addiction had resulted in disciplinary action when he pitched up to work smelling of alcohol. He said this event was the worst and best of times. Worst because it was his rock-bottom and best because he was forced to do something about his using. He said he had met Margot Laird as he was about to graduate from the treatment centre he had been in. She was doing one of her talks and they had got chatting. She gave him her card and said to contact her when he knew what and where he wanted to work. He, first of all, went back to his old job but Margot's words resonated with him, so after a few months he made the move and came to work at Moriatta Falls." It was the best thing I've ever done," he added. "You know this type of job is about the only job where 'ex-addict' or 'recovering addict' to be more precise doesn't carry a penalty. Rehabs know our value."

"Yes," I agreed, "with you knowing how I feel and having been in the same or similar mental states that I got into is actually a comfort and inspiration."

Malc Night Nurse- in his 50's a big bear of a man – A bit scary looking at first but with a very gentle manner, I discovered he was great to have around in times of stress or trouble, Malc could be tough or protective, depending on the need at any given time. He was a solid and comforting person that tended to look out for everyone. As the clinic was in a remote place it was also comforting to have Malc and the other guys around to look out for all of us, especially at night.

Ruby Night Nurse was somewhere in her 20's she was generally the boy's favourite, long dark hair and pretty. She too was a kind of comforting person to have around always able to say the right thing or calm you down after a bloody nightmare. She was always in great demand after dinner, when the long evenings ahead could seem to stretch on forever. She always knew just what to do and say to help with homesickness or to help with bits of work we got stuck over. Ruby said she wasn't an addict but had family members who were. She said she had been to the family support groups and Al-Anon meetings, which both had helped in terms of her family but also the work she did with us.

The night time nurses seemed a lot more relaxed than the daytime crew. They suggested perhaps it was because we had more free time with them, no night groups for instance. Plus everyone was winding down after hard days in group and were more able to chat and idle away some time. The days were more formal with groups, and people to see and speak to, our timetable was very busy. Getting us back into the swing of life after some of us had opted out of it. Once I started group for real, I liked the more timetabled day. Amazing how much we all learnt to like group, fearing it to start with then respecting the power it had over changing the way we thought and felt.

Alan and Malc went on describing what days at the clinic were like. They said, "there were lots of workshops and lectures, Moriatta Falls had a strong belief that education could change the world, or at least an individual," they added smiling. "Tomorrow, for instance, you are going to meet some of the therapy team and there's a lecture planned."

"This sounds quite formal and hard work," I say to them.

"Yep it is hard work coming to a place like this. There is an awful lot to cram into however long your stay is. The more you learn the easier it will be to make changes to your life, and then the easier it will be to change and stay clean and sober."

"To be honest," I said, "I'm not too sure that's what I want, I just want the trouble to stop."

"The trouble," said Malc, "is usually powered by your addiction, the trouble cannot stop unless you decide to stop using."

With those 'sobering' words I returned to my plotting about how to get out to my car to check those dents. I had been shown the group room which was a pleasant enough space. It was painted in calming colours, and had comfortable chairs in a circle, a whiteboard and slogan type things around the walls. The circled chairs were a bit of a worry. Although I had been told that 'the break you down to build you up' did not exist anymore, I was certain this was exactly what would happen in group. The thought still terrified me despite all the positive stuff the nurses said. I also suspected that once group started getting out to the car might be more of a hassle.

"Hey Malc, do you think you could accompany out to my car? I need to get something from the glove box. My bank cards are in there and I need them to pay my deposit."

"Ah, you are staying then?" said Malc.

"Well, just for a while," I said as I tried to smile.

I was instructed to put my coat on and Malc accompanied me out to the car. I unlocked the door and tried without seeming too obvious to check the outside. I got the cards from the glovebox and my heart gave a jump as I noticed the scratches and dents on the passenger side of the car.

Malc caught my gaze and asked me about the damage.

I ran my fingers around the dents making up some stupid story about scraping a tree.

I shoved my hands deeply into my pockets whilst Malc locked the car and took my credit cards.

"I'll keep these in our safe, and you need to go back to bed and try to sleep, you look white as a sheet again."

I returned to my room and slowly took my hands from my pockets. My worst fears were confirmed, I had blood on them, I must have hit something. There was not much blood but definitely enough for me to recognise the red dried flecks under my nails.

I started to cry,

Oh God no, this can't be happening I thought as I tried to come up with a plan to deal with this.

Well I won't say anything to anyone. They'll arrest me for sure. The police haven't called yet, maybe if I stay quiet I will get away with this. I felt sick as I thought about some poor injured, or worse still, some dead person that I had killed.

I have to just stay quiet. I thought, no-one can know.

The staff who had moved my car, hadn't noticed anything wrong. You couldn't miss the dents and scratches, but the blood smears were faint and not much of it.

There was no police alerts or anything on the local news.

Maybe it's nothing I thought trying to convince myself this

was the case.

I'm not going to say anything, I need to get well, bloody hell why do these things always happen to me? Just when I had decided I was going to do something about my using this has to happen.

My self-pity was pretty awesome in these moments, I felt terrible, but I also knew I had to keep quiet or spend the rest of my life in jail. People hate drunk drivers these days. I hate drunk drivers for goodness sake, why the hell do I do these things?

Oh shit, I'll just stay here hidden in this place for a month and hopefully it will all blow over, by the time I get out.

I, at last, went to bed and tried to sleep, tossing and turning as the horrible facts went over and over in my mind.

WORKSHOP
SUICIDE AWARENESS

"Morning everyone, today we are going to talk about Suicide awareness. It's a subject which seems pretty dark, and for some of the new people who come into this lecture it might be a little bit scary. But the information is something everyone knows a little about, some of you may even have contemplated or tried to do it. So our belief is that communication is our strongest ally in protecting you. We heard about the conversation yesterday, Brendon and Aiden, where you talked about the poem Margot wrote and the reason for it, so thought we should fill in some more missing blanks. If anyone is disturbed by this talk, then please let us know. We will give you a lot of facts, so we will take questions and comments at the end of the workshop. But interrupt and comment if you want or need to. We like to be quite interactive."

- **Deaths by suicide are on the rise There are many ways people who want to die like this, plan and execute it. Your illness, addiction, has the reputation of being one of the strongest reasons people end up and then succeeding in dying like this.**
- **The deep dark depressions that some addicts**

fall into of course are the culprits for rationale thinking going astray.
- A human's strongest impulse is to survive, we are born with this impulse.
- We are born crying for oxygen, food, warmth, and love and safety.
- For people to want and plan to die by their own hand is self-harming taken to the extreme.
- It is an indication that something is very wrong with our thinking. Suicidal ideation is taken extremely seriously by anyone in this rehab, but also all who work in the Mental Health industry. Statistics tell us that it is on the rise, especially amongst the young.
- Some of the reasons thinking goes wrong are many and varied:
- Psychological trauma, PTSD, Bullying, Financial fears, Relationship struggles, Anxiety, Stress and Depression, Shame as well as Abuse of any kind, emotional, physical and sexual and of course the spectre of addictions in all of its forms.
- Some of the High-risk factors include:
- Mental Health disorders, Social Phobias, feeling of being a Burden, Major Life Changes and Hopelessness.
- Methods for dying this way are many and varied:

- Taking a cocktail of medications with alcohol, jumping from bridges and buildings, shooting, and hanging. With strangely the most common being hanging.
- Despair and feeling a burden to everyone is the common denominator. Suicide notes will often, if they are written, talk about the writer feeling the world would be better off without them.
- It is called selfish by many, yet this is far from the truth.
- Interestingly, it used to be an illegal act, that has changed as more recognition has evolved. People are no longer prosecuted, so the word 'committing' (suicide) can be erased from our vocabularies.
- It used to be thought that we shouldn't discuss subjects like these as for those who are in this mental dilemma it could encourage you. But that thinking is changing as more research has evolved.
- There is a very interesting piece of information that has been researched in America. Some of you may know the Golden Gate Bridge? This place is a 'famous' jumping-off place, used so often that rescue ships patrol trying to keep an eye out. One incredible survivor speaks openly about, at the second of jumping, he

changed his mind and in that moment he was able to position his body to enter the water in a way that did the least damage, and he miraculously survived. His survival is what many base these type of talks on. He went on to not only survive and recover, but like Margot our founder, travels the world talking about his experience, to help people see that there are many things that could be done in this arena.

- What can we as individuals do?
- Communication and connection are vital. Mood disorders make this the most dangerous of states to be in.
- We should take notice, interfere if we must, give a kind word or two, these kinds of gestures may save a life. Other survivors have spoken about a last-minute change of mind simply because of a kind gesture, a hand on an arm or smile. This shows us that sometimes milliseconds are what separate us from tragedy.
- There has been much research in this area, and it is now thought that talking about, describing and opening up about the most taboo of subjects is the way forward. Our founder is so passionate about this subject that she insists we include workshops and

discussion groups not just for staff but also for patients.

"Ok," said Wolfie "let's open up the discussion, does anyone have anything they want to comment on or ask questions about?"

"Wow!" said Brendon, "talk about baptism by fire for the newbies. That is a dark subject, but I absolutely agree it has to be brought out into the open. I've never got that low but can quite see how it could happen. I've read somewhere that addiction is featured in many successful suicides, so it's a pretty relevant subject."

Rita and Aiden each owned up to having felt like killing themselves, and the common denominator was that at the time each believed as the lecture stated that their family or the world would be better off without them. One had thought about overdose the other by crashing his car into a wall.

I didn't tell them yet that I was part of this gang. I had on several lonely dark occasions contemplated ending it all, and as the lecture had said convinced myself that I was a burden on the world. This stuff with the car was pushing me to a dark place as well.

Rita and Aiden both said they were saddened by the hopelessness they had felt and are glad they had not succeeded.

I didn't know yet if I was glad, but I certainly identified

with feeling sad about how I had ended up feeling. The car stuff was heavy in my mind, but other things that had gone wrong in my life also took centre stage.

No wonder we end up bloody depressed and suicidal I thought.

Others in the group had tales of people they had known who had managed to kill themselves. Wolfie said, that it felt like we were remembering them and their lives and honouring our own feelings. Perhaps talking about their mental states would enable ours to not descend to the same depths, and therefore their tragedy becomes our saving grace. Wolfie said this kind of openness was important and encouraged us to remain open.

"That's a nice way of thinking about such a sad thing," Rita said.

We all agreed that yes this was a difficult and sad topic but were not harmed by the content or by talking about it, the two who had owned up to their desperate feelings also said they were glad to have been able to be so open with a group of people and not feel judged. I just kept shtum, not yet ready to be so open about myself, about this or anything else.

Wolfie gave us with a quote from Martin Luther King Jnr.

Darkness cannot drive out darkness,
Only light can do that.
Hate cannot drive out hate only love can do that.

He said that addictions have such a bad reputation, there are so many myths and misconceptions about this illness. People who use, often die early or get so sick they want to die. It is a lonely awful disease and perceptions about it HAVE to change, if the world is to find better solutions.

The behaviours of out of control addictions are also pretty bad, it's hardly surprising addicts have such a bad press and addicts end up wanting to die, but if perceptions about the illness could change, then perhaps more people could find recovery or not fall into its traps so easily.

I thought about Margot Laird and her quest to bring recovery to people who had contemplated this darkest of deeds.

She must be some woman I thought, creating a treatment centre and going around the world trying to help people. I don't know her, but I like her.

4: Megan, Her Pets, and Pavla

So, to my first day in group, I had met everyone at breakfast, and the medics had all given me the go-ahead to go to group and to start this process of 'group work'. I didn't know what to expect, I was bloody scared. Is it too late to escape? What the hell am I doing here? This crazy refrain went around and round my head, and Amy and her rehab song pops into the mix too. As usual though I say nothing and just tag onto whatever is going down. Trying to make myself small and insignificant, with the thought that If I said nothing maybe they'll leave me alone. The workshop had been a welcome start as all I had to do was listen as the therapists spoke and the rest of the patients called out questions and comments. It was pretty relaxed to be honest, even though it was the most unrelaxing of subjects. Is that a word I thought?

The lecture about suicide breaks the ice, and we are all attentive and interested, even me.

"Well," says Wolfie, "we have a couple of newcomers to the group, so before we get down to today's business lets introduce ourselves telling Mimi and Pete, who we are, why we are here and what programme work we are doing."

A preamble is read out, telling me and the rest that the purpose of group was to find our voices, there's a kind of instruction too about everything being confidential and respectful.

Very formal, I think, seriousness coming into the fray. I guess this is where they start to break me down.

Rita, Brendon and Aiden all say hello and tell me they are here dealing with their addiction, we had met yesterday so felt like I knew them. Megan the pretty student, tells me she is 19 and couldn't stay at University because her mind was affected by her addiction. Pavla smiles and says she is telling her story later so for now all she would say is she is glad to be here. Hamish says he has retired from a life of academia and his drinking got out of control. Again that strange matter of a fact tone that everyone seems to have when talking about addiction and anything else in this place. I can't quite understand how they can all be so open and nonchalant about such serious things. I am left to my own thoughts while group continues.

The two therapists introduce themselves," Hi, I'm Wolfie, Head therapist at Moriatta Falls, I've been here for many years and am in recovery myself."

Surprising, surely he can't be an addict too?

He heaps on the surprises when he goes onto say his drug of choice was Heroin and anything else when he could get it! He was dressed rather flamboyantly today with exceedingly colourful socks.

Interesting I think. Heroin and mad socks.

I'm told later that his socks are legendary, and everyone always tries to find him the maddest look, when presents are given.

How does that fit in with rottweilers and target practice? I wonder.

"Hi, I'm Sindy, working at MF for 2 years and loving every minute of my sobriety. I work closely with family members and will tell you more about the family support group later. I have my own family and a dog and am so grateful to have found some answers to the problems I had in my life. We always tell you that if you are brave enough to do the work we suggest, the best version of yourselves is what we all discover."

I've stopped being surprised by people telling me they are addicts now. Anything goes I think. I like the abbreviation for Moriatta Falls makes it easy. I'm looking out for eyebrows too but suspect the patients have been pulling my leg. I like what she says about the best version of myself but can't really fathom where or what that part of me is.

But oh hell! Now it is my turn. Shit, what do I say? In the end I give a wobbly smile and say I am pleased to be here. More lies, I think. Disconcerted that my voice is still meek and mild.

Pete also looks uncertain, he looks pretty white and ill, so just gives a small smile, waves but says nothing We give each other sympathetic glances, a brother and sister in arms kind of look.

"Well," says Wolfie, "welcome everyone, this morning we have a bit of business to clear up before we can get on with some of the presentations you guys have been working on. As you know we always discuss the clinic and group business and anything else you might need to talk about before any programme work gets done."

"Ok Megan, you know this involves you, would you like to tell the group what happened this morning?"

Megan looks sulky and a little bit scared, "don't really want to tell all these people about my pets. They don't care anyhow, why are you making such a fuss about everything?"

"Come on Meg don't drag this out, you know when you've got the floor you have to speak," says Aiden.

Megan shoots him a venomous look.

Oh not so pretty now, I think, wonder what she did? I swear if Megan were a snake she'd be hissing by now.

"Come on," says Wolfie, "spill the beans. You almost gave our housekeeper Pia, a heart attack this morning, we have to have this out in the open so you and we can move on."

Grudgingly Megan begins to tell the group about her 'pets'.

"I've been collecting spiders now for ages, wherever I go I scoop 'em up and save them from all of you horrible people who hate them. I don't do any harm; I never take the pregnant mothers and I keep them safe in my jars and matchboxes in my bedroom drawers."

Pavla has a stricken look on her face,

"In your room - in your drawers – spiders?"

She runs out of words. Sindy the counsellor and Rita both look as stricken as Pavla who now looks like she is about to faint. Sindy rubs Pavla's back while Rita gets her some water. Sindy's eyebrows seem to be doing the jive! Rising and falling with the expressions on her face, so the patients were telling the truth, but the news we were all hearing did not sound funny at all.

I was beginning to think everyone I was meeting and hearing about was absolutely insane. I did not yet know how right I was.

"Bloody hell," says Aiden, "wasn't expecting that Spider Girl."

"You shut up," says Megan, "I'm not hurting anyone, and I'm actually saving them and being eco savvy. I've been doing this for ages and have quite a collection. I feed them, and label them and nobody gets hurt so why the fuss? I can't help it if you are all arachnophobes."

Wolfie takes control of this rapidly spiralling discussion. "Ok everyone one at a time. Firstly Megan we cannot be seen to be keeping livestock in our facility, spiders, rabbits or anything. Secondly spiders are meant to be free, they are not supposed to be caught and kept in matchboxes and jars or bedroom drawers. Thirdly so many people have phobias about spiders including Pia, who as I said when cleaning your room was surprised at how heavy your chest of drawers felt and then found your zoo. Megan, he said sternly, Pia almost had a heart attack, she refuses to go back into your room until you remove your pets. You will have to let them go and I will help you do this. Everyone else have a ten-minute break." With that he accompanies Megan out to go to her room.

"Bloody hell," says Aiden again, "only in rehab!"

As some of us get up and troop to the smoking shed, which still looks as unsavoury as last night but the nicotine was so welcome after this fright. Pavla is looking decidedly ill now and is being walked around the garden by Sindy.

Well if that's the flavour of group I think to myself, bring it on, it's mad, and I love mad! I say, "is that the flavour of group then?"

I am assured that this was a one-off, and no-one present had ever experienced anything like it. We are usually talking about addiction or recovery; we don't tend to talk spiders. God, poor Pia, I certainly would not have liked to have been her this morning, finding that little fright fest. Someone starts to laugh and before we know it everyone is in hysterics, including Pavla who comes in from the garden, just as Megan and Wolfie are going out to the garden holding a drawer at each end.

Another few minutes go by, while we calm down, finish

our cigarettes and then troop back to the group room, while we wait for Wolfie and Megan. The ice has truly been broken and the feel in the room is as if we have known each other for years and have not just met. Wolfie and Megan then return, and the room settles down. Megan looks sheepish and seems about to cry.

"I'm sorry everyone, didn't mean to upset you all, I just don't understand why everyone hates spiders so much," at which point we all have hysterics again, including the counsellors and Megan.

We eventually settle down and Wolfie takes control of the group, "OK guys he says we can all join in congratulating Megan for bowing to the will of the group and letting her pets go." Megan grimaces and gives a little nod of acceptance.

"Can't help it, Meg you are now going down in legend as Spider Girl. I won't ever forget it," says Aiden as he smiles at Megan.

"My name's Megan," she hisses back.

Not lost the fire then girl, good for you I think.

"Ok now folks we are going to get on with the mornings work which as most of you know will be Pavla's story. For those of you who don't know, an important part of your stay in rehab is to begin to open up and start communicating about some of the things you've done in your addictions and in your life. Talking and opening up is something which all of you need to be able to do to get well. Difficult but necessary.

You will also notice that Pete is not with us, he is feeling ill again and has opted out of this part of group." This news brings our merrymaking to a halt and a hush descends as we all settle down to think about poor Pete and to listen to someone begin their journey in treatment.

Pavla

Okay, Dahrlinks, don't judge me please,

I was born into a hard-working family, my mother and father owned a dress shop in Bulgaria, it was successful, my older brother and I were pretty close as the parents were very often out and about, either at the shop or buying stock, or something like that. My grandmother looked after us mostly, I loved her very much, she made clothes for me and my brother and she was an angel.

I don't remember too much as a little girl except that grandma was the focus of everything. The parents were always at the shop I remember my father drinking quite a bit and my mother and grandmother making sure us children were kept out of the way. He could get quite angry at times and I remember hearing him shout a lot some nights. My mother would be crying and looking sad a lot of the time she was at home. I would just try to ignore his shouting by pulling the covers over my head and pretending I was somewhere else.

I was ten years old when the family moved to Britain. I hated the move; I hated the school I went to and I hated the weather. Sorry dahrlinks, I hated Britain, I remember the kids at my new school being mean to me about my accent. I missed my friends and my grandma who was left behind in Bulgaria. I cried so much about this. My brother was the only friend I had, and he didn't want his baby sister around too much anymore.

I can remember that I stopped eating very much because I always felt sick, The British food was horrible, and I was just so unhappy. No-one really noticed I had stopped eating until some teacher at the school sent a letter home to my parents. They were so busy with their new fashion business in Britain that they had not noticed. It was quite a shock when I ended up at the doctors and was told I had to put on weight or go to hospital. I was twelve and had been diagnosed with Anorexia, I was actually quite ill, I just remember being fed up at everyone telling me what to do. I managed to stay out of hospital by putting on a little weight, eating a bit and by putting stones in my clothes when I was weighed. I got away with it somehow and ate just enough to stay out of hospital. My father's drinking continued to get worse over the years and eventually he left us kids and my mother and ran off with another woman. Actually I think my mother kicked him out but don't really know.

The business was good so financially we were ok. I endured school, then at the age of 16 I was 'discovered' by a company in London who were on the lookout for models. I had grown quite a bit in height and was still pretty skinny, I had managed to make a problem become an asset, so, that's what happened I became a model, and all the girls envied my ability to stay skinny.

I moved to London to pursue my dream of being a supermodel, and started to travel the world with my agency, they were good to me and found me great jobs. Some of the men I worked for were not so good, but you got used to that if you wanted to keep working. This is where I developed my love of amphetamines, they made it even easier to keep the weight down and when I used them with alcohol the 'cocktail' gave me superhuman energy. The photographers were the worst, getting us girls to take too many clothes off when it was not really necessary. You had to keep on your toes to avoid too much trouble with these people. They had all the power though, so we learned how to keep ourselves and each other safe. I earned lots of money and, although never as much as a supermodel, I did alright. As much as I had hated the UK, it has been good to me.

I got sick of it all in the end when I met the man I fell in love with, we decided we wanted to be together without all the travelling, so I left modelling, and we, Marco and I decided to open up an online clothing business. We got very successful very quickly and It felt like I had come full circle. Over the years my drinking seemed to follow the same pattern as my fathers. I drank a lot and too much. The arguments I had with Marco about business and about my weight and about him staying out all night were getting worse and worse. My last binge ended up with me screaming at Marco that I wanted to kill him, the police were called, I was carted off to be detained for the night, they told me I was like a mad dog, and they could not quieten me. Then the next day Marco gave an ultimatum of go to rehab or he would leave me. I still love him so much; I have no idea what made me so mad I threatened to kill him. I don't think I will ever forget the shame of waking up in a police cell. I've had enough of the trouble and the shame; I want to do something about it. – that's it folks, says Pavla – her jaunty ending sounding hollow and insincere after that tale of woe.

Pavla began crying quietly.

Wolfie praised the content, saying, "you kept many of the more lurid incidences of what happened to you out of the story, so will need to do a bit more work. You've also been very modest about your business, we know it is hugely successful, but the next pieces of work you present will enable you to go into more detail about everything. For now, well done, would you like to hear some feedback from your group?"

"Well done Pavla," said Rita, "you were brave in telling us about your eating disorder. I know you don't like to talk about it or how you were bullied at school for your lovely accent. People can be pigs can't they? The patterns in your story are amazing, with the theme of addictions, loss and arguments all taking centre stage."

Hamish, Molly, Aiden and Brendon all spoke a few words of encouragement and praise. I was a bit dumbstruck, but I recognised some of the patterns that emerged in Pavla's story, I could sense some of the pain that she did not actually voice, and her eyes and shaking hands told their own sad story.

"Well done Pavla, that was brave and amazing," I said at last. I thought however, MORE DETAILS? - Hell - They expect a lot!

Wolfie and Sindy went onto say that Pavla was brave for opening up about personal things. They went through different parts of the story and looked at how the events shaped her personality and how her personality and events affected her feelings. Which for an addict was how the illness was able to develop and progress. Pavla had told us how she found something (Anorexia or Alcohol) that helped her cope whenever life got too difficult. A lot of the counsellors' feedback went right over my head, I certainly did not understand how personality and feelings led to addiction. My thoughts were that Wolfie was just being nice to Pavla, everyone knew we did these vile things to ourselves. We didn't have to drink so much or use stupid drugs, we just wanted to get high, or at least that is what I wanted.

As though Wolfie could hear my thoughts he made a point of saying that the DVD which was being played this afternoon would explain in detail more about addiction and its causes. New people were not to worry if they fell asleep as this was a common ritual mostly for newbies and we would have a chance to repeat the film, as this knowledge of the disease concept was vital in order to help us progress. We very often have to repeat DVD's and workshops because your attention spans are limited when you first come into treatment. Often when patients are in detox even the simple task of watching a film proves too much, or too taxing. So we repeat and return to the important things you need to learn in Rehab.

Interesting, I thought, the film sounds like something new for me to get my head around. Let's face it, I know next to nothing about the so-called illness that I have. My interest was certainly being sparked by all the different events and discussions happening as a matter of course around and about this place.

At this point Wolfie said that group was over, and we could have a break, have lunch and to meet up at 2.00. – We all troop out, me exhausted at the story about Spider Girl, and at Pavla's sad tale, and very concerned about Pete.

Wow! Only the first group day, only a morning's work, what else can happen I think? For a very short while my problems with the blood and the car and what to do about it disappeared from my thoughts.

5: 'I'll Do It Tomorrow' Becomes Obsolete

As we all gathered in the TV room to start watching the planned DVD, our happy mood was suddenly interrupted by the sounds of sirens and an ambulance pulling up in the driveway.

At that moment Sindy came into the room and told us not to worry, Pete had become steadily more unwell and had to go to hospital as a precaution. We were silent as we watched Pete being taken out of the clinic by stretcher.

"But he's so young," someone protested. "What's wrong?"

Sindy told us that age had nothing to do with anything, it was more a matter of luck if our bodies coped with what we unthinkingly poured and put into them. Detox is the most dangerous time for addicts. Some people's constitutions were stronger than others, plus the type of drinking and drugging that Pete had engaged in had been heavy, plus he had not really looked after himself. She added that we would be hearing lots of lectures about the harm our lifestyles could have on our bodies and that the film this afternoon went into more detail about what was really wrong with us.

Reality hits, thinks I, this is really serious shit, feeling worried for Pete and worried for myself.

"Don't worry Blue," says Brendon, "we'll look after you."

"What's this 'blue' thing you keep saying?" I ask.

"It's just something we say to describe a redheaded beauty like you, he replies. Don't ask, it's complicated!"

I smile at Brendon's compliment as I know he is just trying to lighten the mood.

We settle down to be educated about what is really wrong with us. Hamish falls asleep immediately and Aiden starts breaking out the chocolate and sweets. Megan curls up into a little ball in her chair but stays alert. Brendon, I, Rita and Pavla all settle down as well, refusing the sweets Aiden offers.

I like the American accent of the presenter, always have always will, that was the last irrelevant thought I had in the next hour. The DVD started to describe this illness of addiction in a way I had never heard before.

- **It talked about the brain and how the behaviours engaged in, created abnormal spikes of different chemicals in our systems. Dopamine and Serotonin were the chemicals that I remember him talking about.**
- **These chemicals are powerful, becoming something our systems crave and believe it needs, not just wants. This need for the stimulus that is provided by our substances and behaviours climbs up the scale of survival**

needs and becomes the number one survival instinct in addicts. This bit of our thinking process goes wrong. It can't be seen; flawed thinking shows through 'behaviour'.

- **In the percentage of people who are classified as addicts this is the thing that sets them apart from people who do not abuse substances or have any of the other behavioural addictions.**
- **Addicts are different. Processing things differently in body and mind. The thinking is flawed as the mind/brain begins to believe that using is not just a want or a choice but an actual need. Addicts have to learn how addiction hijacks the brain, in order to understand how to manage the illness.**

Makes sense now I think, of all the times I promised my mother, myself, and everyone, I will not do it again, and then promptly do it again as I try to cover up my vile behaviours with lies, unable to live up to my promise.

- **Over time it is impossible to halt what is going on without intervention or treatment such as we were having at MF. Remember the progressive nature of the disease. Something other than self has to intervene in order to halt the progression. We cannot do this ourselves. Abstinence has to start the process.**

- **At this stage Abstinence is the last thing any of us want. We have become obsessive and compulsive about the things we use and do.**
- **It is serious consequences that 'force' us to get honest about what is going on.**
- **This is well documented by scientists and the medical profession; research continues about this disease. There is no cure, but it is manageable, once you find the right formula. This is what is taught in Rehab, and Recovery rooms everywhere.**
- **We are not to blame, it is not our fault that we have the disease, but it is our responsibility to do something about it once we know.**

Shame the rest of the world doesn't believe this I think.

Dire comments such as there is no cure and the statistics about death by addiction were talked about at length.

We are all quiet, taking in the information, Brendon and Aiden are taking notes, Hamish is snoring gently, not loud enough for us to be disturbed but enough to tell us he was fast asleep. The rest of us were listening intently to the information given. The film ends.

"Why isn't this mainstream knowledge?" I ask.

"Well it is, and it isn't," says Brendon, "the medical world and others have known about this forever, the problem comes I think in how it is to be treated. This place and others like it, believes Abstinence is the only way, other models of treatment think we can be taught to drink like gentlemen and women, they only say that about alcohol though, coke and speed etc are illegal so they don't dare tell us to use like gents and ladies! Plus how on earth do you gamble like a gentleman or lady?"

Ridiculous when you say it that way, I think.

Aiden then chips in with, "The World Health Organisation says if alcohol were a drug discovered today it would be a Class A, illegal and dangerous."

Rita says, "more alcoholics die than with any other substance." We all immediately think of Pete and hope he is ok.

The conversation is interesting with lots of facts and never before known things about alcohol and drugs and addiction and treatment.

"The therapists will begin to fill in the missing bits as you get going in treatment. Stick around Mimi you will learn lots," says Brendon, "but for now just remember 'our best thinking got us here!' This is something the therapy team remind us of all the time. Annoys me to be honest, but it's so true. That and that bloody 'honesty is a prerequisite to recovery' saying."

I can see that I already have learnt lots, this addiction stuff is more serious than I ever thought, and I really do have to stay to sort it out. With every passing moment in this place

I am realising that one of my favourite sayings of 'sorting this out tomorrow' will have to change. Maybe if I leave it too long there might be no more tomorrow, I realise as Pete's white face swims into my mind. I don't want to end up like him, so although I'm not thrilled to be here at the clinic, I know I have to be here. I am left wondering about the saying 'our best thinking got us here'

We all troop out, some into the garden for a quick cigarette, some to the nurses' station, I go to my room, exhausted once again by all this new information I am processing. All these people I am talking to. The real world seems to have diminished and the world at Moriatta Falls has taken centre stage. Not too shabby a world I think, at least there is some nice eye candy to look at as Christophe floats into my mind.

So pathetic girl, my head tells me, getting wound up in trivialities and irrelevancies does not become you. I can hear my mother saying these words, as I mentally admonish myself.

And then as if by magic Christophe pokes his head into my room and asks if I am alright to do some of the paperwork still needing to be done.

"Please do come in," I say, secretly pleased at the distraction this will give me. I ask about Pete and how he is, Christophe says seriously "Pete is pretty unwell he won't be back tonight."

I tell Christophe "I am shocked at the news that Pete is so

ill." Christophe says "it happens quite a lot, more often to the more elderly whose bodies are frailer, but sometimes as in Pete's case his lifestyle has contributed to the status quo. We will let everyone know when and if he is to return."

I tell Christophe that "I hadn't realised alcohol could cause such a reaction; I had thought it was only the more dangerous things like Heroin etc that we had to be careful about." Christophe said "everyone actually believes that, but all drugs can and will kill you if the disease progresses enough, but it is the withdrawal effect in alcoholism that create the worst kind of symptoms. You can experience things such as fits or seizures for instance in detox. The other really weird thing for me," says Christophe, "is that alcohol is legal and everything else practically is illegal. Another one of those strange anomalies in the land of addiction. Alcohol can kill you very fast yet is legal and used just about everywhere for everything. Births, deaths, marriages. We as a society need to rethink some of the strange things that go on in our world, there should not be a substance that can kill so quickly and be obtained so easily and cheaply."

"No," I reply, "When you put it like that it doesn't make much sense, but can you imagine the shitstorm if the stuff was banned or made more difficult to buy? There are ructions if alcohol is put up in price, let alone if it were banned."

It seems every conversation, every interaction is a learning curve in this story of addiction. I tell Christophe "I had not realised I was so ignorant about things."

He said "unfortunately where addiction is concerned there is way too much ignorance, not enough understanding. – well young lady, this is what you have come here to do, so try to enjoy your lessons!"

Secretly happy he has called me a young lady I settle down and finish the paperwork he has brought with him.

Dinnertime that evening is a lively affair, with Pete, Spider Girl, Pavla and the real reason we are all at the clinic as topics of conversation, even Hamish is livelier and joins in. I realise this is the first time in a long time that my head is active and questioning and involved in life, rather than being dulled and preoccupied in pursuit of the elusive highs I have believed I wanted. I realise too that those highs are milliseconds in duration, a great feeling of course but really as soon as it is felt it disappears either into blackout or some other degrading thing. But who can ignore those cravings? I think this as I realise I haven't had any.

"Can someone explain the 'my best thinking got me here'" says Megan, who has become quite docile now that the spiders have been set free and no-one seems to be judging her weird behaviour.

"Well," says Brendon, "I would say I'm a pretty smart resourceful kind of person. I'm not banging my own drum, but I've done alright in the world. With no help from anyone I have built a business which is very successful. From all our midnight chats around the campfire, we have all told each other bits about ourselves, so I know for instance that Rita has done all right in the music biz and has a grown-up family, and look at Pavla, she and her husband also have been successful in their line of work, Hamish is an academic, Aiden for heaven's sake against all the odds you became a chef, Megan you're at University etcetera, so no problem with our brains in that department, yet here we all are, brought to our knees by an illness none of us saw coming. In my case I did some pretty dumb things in pursuit of my drug of choice, felt the consequences, yet did it again and again. My thinking when it came to my addiction was pretty twisted. Ergo my best thinking when it came to my addiction got me here!"

The discussion grew livelier with everyone chipping in their thoughts and owning up to insane thoughts about themselves and their lives.

I'm learning, I think to myself happily, as I let the sounds of Moriatta Falls and my new companions wash over me. If only the mystery of the bloody car could be solved, I could relax and even like it here. But I'm not going to do anything, silence is the best method in situations like this. No-one can know. There had been no news bulletin's, so I felt quite sure no-one was searching for me and my car.

6: Rules, Regulations and Taming the Rebels

1. Alcohol, drugs, prescription medications as well as any other addictive behaviours are forbidden in treatment. If you are caught engaging in any of them you could be discharged.
2. There are random drug tests, if you refuse them you could be discharged.
3. Intimate relationships will not be tolerated, staff will remind you to socialise as a group if you refuse you could be discharged.
4. If you are found in another person's bedroom you will be discharged.
5. You will be allowed out once the medical team agree you are fit, you can only go out accompanied by others in the group. You MUST stick together.
6. You cannot go out after 6.00pm at night, you can only go out accompanied.
7. You cannot go out in each other's cars, your car keys should be handed in.
8. Please don't bring sugary carbonated drinks in from your walks to the shops, your bags will

be searched and all the 'forbidden' things removed and disposed of.
9. You can only smoke in the designated areas, if you are caught smoking anywhere else you risk discharge.
10. Gambling, gaming, pornography online dating, drinking strong coffee and excessive use of your mobile phones can be seen as addictive practices and need to be stopped or regulated. You must only use your mobile after the working day.
11. We ask that you treat others as you wish to be treated, aggression to staff or other patients will not be tolerated, and you could be discharged.
12. HONESTY is the pre-requisite to Recovery.

Wolfie and Ellen are running group today and start with that list of rules.

Ellen says she is training to be a therapist and is going to University to study addictions. She adds that she used to be a patient here some years ago. I have heard her tell bits of her story before and the 'I used to be a patient here' always interests everyone. She gets lots of questions about all sorts of things such as the life stories of the other therapists, which she doesn't ever tell us.

We have been going to different meetings, some outside

the clinic once our detoxes are over, but the majority are internal. We are beginning to meet lots of other recovering addicts who have managed to stop using. The ex-patients of MF are always the more interesting of people and we tend to gravitate towards them, like members of our own extended families. All this interaction makes the 'journey' in the clinic more bearable and the thought of recovery more possible. It is not just the facility telling us these things to make us believe it, but real live people, some having done what we are now doing and all of them trying to become or stay clean and sober. I have met, all sorts of addicts, from the usual alcoholics and drug addicts, to gamblers, and people with eating disorders, to shopping addiction, and sex addiction and all of the things spoken of in our rules and regulations. They come from all walks of life as well. This really is an education like no other.

No stereotypes in this place, I thought. Just as this thought came, I had several 'lightbulb' moments at once. The stereotypical idea about alcoholics and addicts was the reason I didn't think I was one. I did not live on a park bench, I did not drink or use daily, I did not have the shakes, and lots of other things 'I did not have'.

After Ellen reads out the rules and regulations she asks if there are any comments or questions.

"Can anyone tell me what a definition of addiction is?" I ask.

"Great question," says Ellen, and writes up on the

whiteboard the following:

ADDICTION = A RELIANCE ON A SUBSTANCE OR BEHAVIOUR IN ORDER TO CHANGE THE WAY WE FEEL

As we think about this answer we can all see how this fits just about every scenario we cared to think about: To get happy or happier, to de-stress, to comfort or compensate. Our drug of choice, substance or behaviour, becomes the go-to thing for a multiple of reasons.

"Understanding this definition also helps you understand why 'feelings' are such a hot topic in therapy," says Ellen.

Aiden raises a question about the 'intimate relationships?'

"It is what it implies Aiden, no fraternising!" She smiles as she says it to soften the harsh word. "We have had some experiences of people becoming too involved and it has never had a good outcome so we remind you often to stick to being 'a group' You can easily misunderstand relationships in a place like this, the work we do gives the illusion of intimacy, but it is false because of course you have only just met. The other thing that should halt any get-togethers is the fact that sobriety is hard-won and needs to be the most important thing in your life. Love affairs are the quickest way to lose focus, or to avoid painful reality. If you are single you should not entertain the idea of a relationship for at least a year, and if you are already in a relationship, good or bad you need to work on the one you have to either heal it or end it cleanly with care and respect. Our family therapist Sindy will discuss more about the damage done to relationships and families when she is next in group."

Ellen then says, "to end this part of group I want to read you out something I found."

> **You will teach them to fly but
> They will not fly your flight.**
>
> **You will teach them to dream,
> But they will not dream your dream.**
>
> **You will teach them to live,
> but they will not live your life.**
>
> **Nevertheless,
> In every flight, in every life in every dream
> The print of the way you taught them will remain.**
>
> *- Mother Theresa*

"We always read this out after the rules and regulations as it can feel like we are trying to curb your freedom or your individuality. We are not, we are trying to protect you from yourselves a lot of the time. We want you to be free and to live the best versions of yourself. Addicts are impulsive, and irrational, unthinking of the consequences and often don't realise exactly the trouble they are getting themselves into, some people rebel in treatment, and for everything we have just read out we have examples of the dire consequences of not sticking to the rules."

So the discussion develops around rules and regulations and rebels and toeing the line. We learn that the programme is also known as 'a programme of change' the change part being the most difficult of things. We have to learn what to do with thought patterns and decisions that lead us to use the way we do time after time, despite catastrophic consequences. We sincerely have to want to change, as 'checking out our thinking' with others from the programme is tedious and not something we are used to doing. Addicts apparently are pretty stubborn and self-willed people.

"Pretty dumb as well," I offer, "as I have so many examples of doing the same thing again and again expecting it to be different."

"Yeah," says Brendon, "that is actually a well-known definition of Insanity!"

"I don't want to change THAT much," says Megan, "I just want to stop using drugs so I can go back to Uni. One year of being celibate – you must be joking."

"Well," says someone, "in order to stop doing the drugs, you have to change an awful lot of who you mix with, how you socialise and live. It's a big job and it 'isn't easy. How else do you imagine you can change the way you think?"

Megan looks unconvinced, "well no relationships for a year, you must be nuts! Who is going to do that?"

Just at that moment Wolfie enters the room.

"So sorry to interrupt group, we don't usually interrupt, but I have some serious news I need your help with. As you know Pete was taken off to hospital because his detox was not going well, and he needed some extra care and attention."

"Yeah how is he?" says Brendon.

"Well unfortunately that's what we don't know and why I have interrupted, Pete took off last night, just got dressed and left hospital without anyone seeing him. We and the police want to know if anyone knows where he might have gone? He did not make it back to his own home or here, and as it was very cold last night so we are all worried about where he might have spent the night."

No-one knew anything, Pete had barely made it to group and none of us had a chance to speak with him very much. The thought of freezing nights and sick Pete, however, brought a feeling into group I had never felt before about a stranger, a feeling of dread and fear.

"The police are out looking for him as we speak, if anyone knows anything just come and let us know. I'm sorry to have interrupted with such scary news but it's important to find Pete as soon as we can. I think you should have a break now. Try not to worry and we will let you know if we hear anything new."

The silence and the dread followed us out to the garden, no banter today, we smoked and sat in silence, each of us lost in our own thoughts.

Megan started to cry and said, "I can't stand this," and went to find a nurse.

I followed her and went to my room. I was shivering and feeling sick again. I guess the word insanity really does fit just about everything I was hearing about, I thought again.

Bloody hell Mimi, I thought, you are getting a crash course in some serious shit. I remembered my and Pete's sympathetic looks to each other only a few hours ago and I wished I had taken more time to get to know him.

Everyone I had met so far, both patients and staff have been ok people. The addicts in this place whom you would never know were addicts without listening to their stories, were so out of control. It's all hidden though I thought. I wondered about that and then remembered what someone had said about addiction being a progressive disease. I remembered my thoughts about stereotypes and how I had never been able to accept I was an addict because I wasn't in the gutter, I had never been to jail, I didn't have a dirty mac and secret bottles in it. Those were the stereotypes that everyone associated with this illness, but as I had been told is just one of the stages we can get to if the disease is not treated.

As I was arguing with my thoughts about reaching the gutter, I remembered my shame about some of the stunts I had pulled when under the influence. I suddenly remembered my car again and thought, most likely a murderer too. Oh God it cannot get any worse than that.

I think what I discovered in these moments were that I had reached my worst gutter place and I had no desire to progress it any further.

I wondered for the hundredth time, why oh why hadn't I known that addiction was a disease? This gap in my knowledge was the reason for the reluctance to do something about it. I also wondered that if I had known would I have done something about it sooner? A question without an answer. With the current reputation that addictions have, I suspected not. My shame kept me silent and the problem a secret. The perfect place for addiction to grow.

What am I going to do about my car? I thought for the millionth time. The thought just went round and round. The fear kept me awake at night and my imagination conjured all sorts of nastiness. I prayed for the hundredth time, "please if anyone is listening, I promise not to use again if you get me out of this fix."

We'd heard lectures about the need for honesty, that truth sets you free, I was terrified that if anyone knew the truth I'd most certainly get locked up. So much for setting me free. I knew something had to be done about all of this, the mad thoughts were tormenting me. But who could I trust with this stuff?

Who wouldn't just call the police and have me taken away? No, best just to shut up and get on with things the best way that I could.

INFORMATION

Addiction as a Disease

World Health Organization – www.who.int/terminology

Defines the dependence syndrome as being a cluster of physiological behavioural cognitive phenomena in which the use of substances or a class of substances takes on a much higher priority for a given individual than other behaviours that once had greater value.

www.NICE.org.uk

Guidelines cover using psychosocial interventions to treat people with problems or are dependent on addictive substances.

www.Merriam-Webster.com

A compulsive, chronic, physiological or psychological need for a substance, behaviour or activity having harmful effects.

www.Addictionreporter.com

Description of Addiction DSM – V which is the diagnostic manual of Mental Disorders which Treatment Professionals identify and treat people affected by addictions.

Dr Steven M Melemis, MD -
www.IWant ToChangeMyLife.org

'I want to Change my Life' – Modern Therapies

Addiction and Recovery – A disease of the wiring of the brain.

Addictive Thinking – Understanding Self-deception
Abraham J Twerski MD – Book

Pleasure Unwoven Kevin Macauley – DVD

7: Aiden, His Lost Digits, and Pete

Aiden starts his story by excusing what he was about to say.

I'm sorry folks my story is not pretty, I grew up in a rough neighbourhood, my old man was out working most of the time and my mother the old cow, looked after us. Well not so much looked after us, but just put up with us. Don't look so upset ladies I'm sorry but you will understand why I hate her so much. I had two siblings and we pretty much did whatever we wanted. My mother was busy in her own life, she liked shopping and was out spending Dad's money at every opportunity. To say we were a wild bunch would be an understatement. We were always in trouble at school, as the oldest, my mother made it my responsibility to look out for the other two, and when they got into trouble she punished me for their misdemeanours.

She was bloody violent and mean, for instance, once my dad bought us a dog, but she refused to feed it and kept telling us to leave it outside as it stank of dog. It didn't matter how much the dog cried she wouldn't let it in the house. In the end I gave the dog away as I could see she was about to do to the dog what she was doing to me. She beat me with an old stick she kept by the sofa, if I ever did anything to upset the applecart I got hit with this stick. She seemed to love hitting me and finding any excuse to do it. I loved my siblings and tried to protect them but in the end I couldn't take her abuse anymore. When I was 16 I ran away from home.

I started busking on the streets of Manchester, made quite a good living as it happens. I met up with a girl called Naomi and we started a life together. We both liked music and parties and living wild. Things were ok for a while, but our lifestyle was always pretty chaotic. Naomi had family money and I made quite a bit out on the streets and in some of the clubs we frequented. Never knew what she saw in me to be honest, but hey I was not going to kick her out of bed. We started to deal cocaine. We both used lots of the stuff and anything else that was available. Any money I made went straight up our noses. Somewhere in this mad world I had decided that I wanted to learn how to be a cook. In some of my enforced slavery at home I had discovered that I liked cooking and was good at it, so that's what I did. I started working in a restaurant. Amazingly I was talent-spotted and was able to go to college and pass some exams, in the end I ended up a pretty decent chef with a pretty decent job. Unfortunately into this happy scene arrived some pretty dark people, my other job of dealing drugs was becoming a bit of a liability. I wanted to leave this part of my life behind, but the money and the coke kept dragging me back.

My lucrative side-line got me caught up in a turf war of sorts with the local gangs, I had always managed to stay independent, but these guys were on a mission to take over Manchester. They, first of all, invited me to join them, then when I refused started to threaten me. I've always had a belief in my own power to look after myself but underestimated the ruthlessness of these people. One night I was ambushed by some of the gang members, taken to an empty building where they began to wield knives and machete's to try to intimidate me, well they did that alright I was shit scared, but never thought they would actually do anything. The threatening bullshit went on for hours, them getting more and more coked up and crazy mad and me trying to make myself small and insignificant. It didn't matter by this time what I said or promised, they were just 'having fun'. In the end to make a longer story short what finished this episode was one of those bastards took one the machetes that they were playing with and cut off two of my fingers, screaming 'there you go chef boy'. I passed out and woke up in hospital, they had dumped me outside of one thankfully otherwise I would have bled to death. A message followed, saying if I was seen to be dealing any more drugs, or speaking to the cops it would not be just two fingers I would lose. Aiden held up his left hand again to show the stumps he had been talking about.

There was a hush in the room as we all took in this ghastly story.

"Oh God Aiden that's so terrible, I never knew things like that happened in real life," whispers Megan.

"Believe you me," said Aiden, "I have toned things down for your delicate ears. Things were much worse, and when Naomi and I took stock we decided I had to go to rehab, get clean and we both had to get out of Manchester. I'm not a gangster or a tough guy and I certainly want to keep all the rest of my digits as well as my life."

We each offered Aiden our support in our own way. Megan jumped up and hugged him, Brendon clapped him on the back. I was horrified at his tale.

More reality checks I thought. God I honestly thought things like this only happened in movies. I have had a very protected life I thought. First his ghastly mother and childhood and then the dark drug world, which we all think we know but don't really.

The therapists wound things down again and ushered us out for a quick break. We were all hushed and contemplative when Aiden says, "Hey gang look!"

As if on cue the police have arrived. We took in this news and went back to the group room some giving Aiden curious looks. My heart skipped several beats, this is it, I thought.

"It's not about me," said Aiden, "the police were not involved, I'm stupid but don't have a death wish. We just upped and left town, no-one knows where I am except Naomi."

Wolfie, Ellen and Sindy, all then come to the group room

looking serious. The room went silent very quickly as we looked at our therapists. We could tell something was seriously amiss. With the echoes of Aiden's story in our heads we were all pretty serious anyway.

"Please don't be alarmed, but we have some shocking news. We are so sorry to have to tell you this, but Pete has been found, although he had been alive when the police got to him, being out last night in the cold was too much for his body and he has passed away."

"Do you mean dead?" shrieks Megan.

The rest of us gasp, silenced by the horrible news.

My heart soared and sank in quick succession, happy it was not about me, but disgusted at my selfishness because it was about Pete.

"Yes I'm afraid Pete has died, his family have been contacted, and the police have arrived to let us know. It was a staff decision to allow you to hear the news from us, to avoid speculation or confusion." Wolfie paused to enable us to digest the news.

"Pete died of hypothermia and addiction. He had left a letter saying he couldn't live like this anymore. This had been his third rehab and this time it was too painful; he knew he would not be able to stay clean. He had voices in his head all the time telling him to give up it would not work. He left our telephone number and asked us to tell you he was sorry; he didn't want to be a burden to you who were new to rehab. He deliberately bought bottles of booze and with a cocktail of alcohol and paracetamol, he settled down in a car he broke into. Wound the windows down, became very cold very quickly and then became unconscious, which was how he was found. The paramedics were unable to resuscitate him. Pete was blue lighted to hospital but never regained consciousness. He died soon after reaching hospital."

Once again we were shocked and subdued. The atmosphere in the room was heavy and sombre. We were hushed and lost.

"What a fucking morning," said Brendon, Megan was crying again. The rest of us stayed silent.

"How can this happen, how could you let this happen?" Rita cried.

"Rita, we did not let this happen, you have to remember you are all here voluntarily, we don't force people to be here, each of you has to want to be here and to make recovery work you have to start learning how to live without drugs and alcohol. Some of your lifestyles are very damaging. Remember this is not the first stop for most of you but could be the last. Nobody ever arrives in rehab because life has been going fantastically, there are a million reasons for ending up in a place like this, none of them happy or good."

"Yeah so some of those rules and things we heard about earlier are little things in comparison to the news of Pete's suicide by addiction, and Aiden's grizzly tale of turf war and drugs." Adds Rita.

"Shit, I got here just in time," I say out loud. "But I'm scared now, I don't want this anymore. I don't want to end up like Pete, with voices telling me recovery is not worth fighting for. I want something else for myself."

"Amen," say Rita and Hamish.

8: Hamish and Running from the Law

Hamish looked decidedly uncomfortable but said, I know I have to do this so I'll just blurt it all out the best way I can.

I've been at the clinic for about 2 weeks now and they have been the most enlightening two weeks of my life. I know I don't join in as much as some of you younger ones, but I feel quite reserved and definitely ashamed of being here at my age.

I have been a science professor and part-time astrologer for all my adult life. My childhood was great, I really have no excuse for ending up an addict in a rehab at the age of 67. I'm married and have 4 grown-up children. We are comfortably off, and anyone looking at our lives would think that it was perfect. It has been pretty good, had its up's and downs of course like anyone else. I loved my job and enjoyed teaching and the students I taught. I have always drunk alcohol, sometimes quite heavily, but my drinking was just some evenings and weekends. It never seemed to cause problems, although I'm not sure my wife would say the same because she often complained about my missing events or sleeping in.

My real issues with alcohol began when I was nearing retirement age, about 2 years ago. I stupidly went into a University lecture with the smell of alcohol on my breath and one of the students reported me. I managed to placate the Principal and told her that I had never done anything like this before and I would not again, I blamed it on a family get together not realising the day after I still smelt of alcohol. I had a frank honest talk with the Principal who said she wanted to believe that it had been a mistake. From then on my drinking just seemed to become more heavy, and I could never keep it under control, I took lots of time off work because I couldn't risk being caught at University again with alcohol on my breath. I was relieved when I eventually retired, I thought I had been clever and avoided trouble, but just before I was admitted here I was caught having driven my car over the limit. I was involved in a massive collision with a brick wall, my car was written off. No-one was hurt thank goodness, but I left the scene of the crime, before the police arrived. I knew if they had breathalysed me I would be in serious trouble. Everyone at home knew I had been drinking but there was no proof for the police to charge me with. They knew too, Hamish said with the first signs of embarrassment, but all they could do was set a court date and tell me I had some explanations to give. They said I would most likely lose my licence and be fined, for leaving the scene of an accident.

My wife was angry with me and said it was the last straw, that I had to go to rehab, or she would tell the police herself that I had been drinking. My children are all angry with me too, and I'm actually furious with my wife for not letting sleeping dogs lie.

"Well done Hamish, that is the most I have heard you say since coming to group," said Wolfie, "before I ask everyone to give you feedback I need to just give you some new things to think about regarding your addiction."

"First of all addiction is usually chronic which means that it has a long life, there is a start to problem drinking, a middle stage and the end stage. It is sometimes not seen as addiction at the start because it is a progressive illness and the more severe problems only show themselves later on in the progression. In your case Hamish, you are saying it only really created massive problems 2 years ago as you neared retirement. Usually with that stage of life, the discipline most scholars have is relaxed a bit as you prepare for more free time and have a less timetabled lifestyle, so your drinking may very well have increased. Your family however may see this story a little bit differently. Addicts live in a perpetual state of denial a lot of the time. Whilst for you, the episode with the Principal and the car crash were consequences you could no longer ignore, it was the end of the line for your wife who gave you an ultimatum, which is why you are here. You said there were no reasons from your childhood experiences to have become addicted, however, this illness does not need 'reasons' to emerge. So some people have wonderful childhoods others have very difficult ones, both sets of circumstances have their own challenges but the thing that creates addiction is in your genes. This is not just 'rehab speak' but information from the latest research about addiction. There is a genetic component to the illness which requires a host i.e. you, and usage to make it explode in your life. The explosions are short and sharp like Megan's or long and slow like yours. It took years for your usage to get really out of control it seems. Perhaps when you really take a hard look at this progression in your life I wonder if you will still have the same thoughts about how long it has been active and troublesome. The anger that your wife and children express appear to tell a very different reality to yours. Remember family members are usually in the frontline for very much longer than anyone else, and they don't actually have blackouts and lapses in memory like we do."

Bloody hell I thought, Hamish has just had the stuffing knocked out of him, Wolfie thinks he's still in denial and not seeing things very clearly. I had to agree with the therapist and after all Hamish had slept all through the DVD which gave me information where I had begun to change my mind about some of the story of addiction.

Hamish drew himself up to his full height of 5ft 11 ins and swore at Wolfie. His face was puce and the veins in his neck were huge. "How dare you, you jumped up little Nazi. I've just put my heart out for all to see and all you can do is to imply I am not telling the truth." Hamish was apoplectic, shaking and spitting venom at Wolfie. "I'm a well-respected professor in my field, I don't have to stay and listen to your views on my life. I've dined with heads of state for Christ's sake. I won't let a little two-bit fool like you who works in a pathetic country clinic tell me I'm not seeing things clearly. How dare you? You'll be hearing from my lawyers." With that Hamish swept out of the room.

The atmosphere in the group room was heavy.

We all looked at each other in silence, wondering what on earth had happened. Wolfie told us not to be concerned, that breaking through denial could be difficult and painful for everyone concerned. "Leave Hamish to the therapy team. Everyone go and have lunch." "Flipping heck! I don't think I can take much more of this. Is rehab always like this? Aren't you upset being called a Nazi?" My surprise at events made me bold and ask questions.

Wolfie smiled at me and said, "we therapists are sometimes called a lot worse. As for rehab being like this, yes, you have to remember we are dealing with a Mental Health Illness not a sore throat or flu symptoms. Everyone makes their own way in rehab, sometimes it is a quick realization and sometimes opinions never change. Hamish is old school, he has been thinking and acting a certain way for many years, he apparently has got away with much bad behaviour over this lifetime, and the victims of his actions as well as his anger are his students, his colleagues at work and of course his long-suffering family. If Hamish stays in rehab and does not run away we can help change his mind, but he is at a crossroads now and he needs to decide about how he wants to proceed."

With Hamish's anger ringing in our ears we troop out of

group and congregate in the smoking shed.

"Never gets any prettier in here does it?" says Aiden. "We should get some paints and do this place up or something."

"Or stop smoking," I say. "But what do you think Hamish is going to do?"

"Well, whatever he does let's hope he does it somewhere warm, I don't think I could take another fatality," says Megan.

"No chance Wolfie got it wrong is there?" says Pavla.

"Hardly," says Brendon, "I think Hamish has been blagging it since he arrived, another example of someone's best thinking, playing tricks. Remember he slept through most of the DVD's and never once sat with us at night. Thought he was too good for us I'd say. Wolfie was spot on as usual."

"Hey," says Rita who although never smokes, always joins in our smoking den. "We've got a lecture planned in the next few days, all about anger. They might bring it forward now that we've all witnessed Hamish having a strop."

"Well just in time," says Aiden, "I'm having a tough time at the moment trying to keep it all together to be honest, just about everything pisses me off. Being able to talk to the staff has been a bit of a lifesaver to be honest, just talking seems to keep that fire in a manageable place thank goodness."

"Well, I'm exhausted as usual," I say, sucking nervously on my cigarette, "I wish I could give these bloody things up too, why don't they ban cigarettes?"

"The belief is," said Brendon, "that addicts cannot deal with that much stress or pressure, smoking is equally destructive to the human body of course, but smokers don't tend to get in cars and mow down innocent people or get into scenes like Aiden described, so the need to quit can seem less necessary."

The comment by Brendon about mowing down people hits me in the solar plexus, and I feel sick and shaky again.

"What's wrong Mimi?" says Rita, who as usual has accompanied us out to the disgusting smoking sheds, "you've gone white as a sheet again."

"Just feeling exhausted again, so much goes on all the time, I feel I can't catch my breath. Pete keeps going through my head and Hamish's angry rant really scared me, reminds me of my old man."

"Wow, well done Mimi," says Brendon, "that's the most intimate bit of your story you've given us yet."

"Yeah I know," I say, "this opening up stuff does not come naturally to me, sorry."

"Well your turn will come soon enough," says Rita, "thinking about it all the time is worse than doing it I promise."

"Thanks Rita," I smile at her attempt to make me feel

better, if only you all knew I thought, you wouldn't be so nice to me then, as the car and the blood resonated in my head like a bad film on endless repeat.

WORKSHOP
THE ANGRY DISEASE

Addiction is known as 'The Angry Disease'.

Many Addicts don't know they are angry or deny it because Anger has a 'reputation'.

In treatment we have to discover many feelings, Anger and how to express it being one of them.

Detox and early recovery brings out this feeling in many.

If you don't realise you will get very angry, you may feel ambushed.

Others can feel attacked by your harsh words and actions.

What is Anger?

It is a natural human emotion, which everyone feels.

It is either Constructive or Destructive depending on how it is used.

Addicts tend to use Anger badly, denying it until it becomes an unstoppable force.

We learn about emotions from our families, at school, our friends, and the media.

Children tend to learn by observation, so if anger is observed to be used destructively this is how we will also use it.

The media shows us a world full of destructive anger.

Some of us have been bullied or become a bully at school.

Anger can be imagined like a volcano, with events being the layers that make up the core, this stacks up with layers of frustration, irritations or annoyances, which in of themselves seem harmless, however too many and they are hard to suppress.

These layers can be seen as 'the here and now', but we have other layers of unexpressed anger such as the events in our addictive lifestyles and our family of origin histories.

Before treatment these have rarely been discussed or worked through.

All of these layers are what addicts usually come into treatment with. Some types of drugs also add to the toxic mix. Detoxing from all of the substances of abuse as well as addictive behaviours always brings up the emotion of anger.

One of the tasks of treatment is to teach you how to talk about all of your feelings especially anger.

Anger is rated as the number one reason for relapse.

Different mediums such as writing, communication, yoga, acupuncture, proper sleep and nutrition, and introducing a timetabled lifestyle are all beneficial in helping to tame anger.

It helps if you, the patient WANT to do this work and start to heal the problems between you and other people.

Staying clean and sober and engaging in the programme of recovery goes a long way in healing some of the chasms between you and the rest of the world.

Learning how to communicate and connect with others who think like us is one of the most important things we learn in treatment.

9: Comings and Goings and Brendon's Deception

We find out pretty soon that Hamish has decided to leave treatment. He had a long session with the therapy team but would not back down from his outraged stance. He does not say goodbye, just up and leaves. Threatening to write letters of complaint to all and sundry. We find out later that his wife has refused to have him home and he has gone to stay in a hotel.

"This story has not ended here," says Brendon, "mark my words, something else will happen to and about Hamish."

"None of us knew him too well he didn't join in any of the events or conversations outside of group, I didn't like him anyway," says Megan, "he gave me the creeps."

The most interesting thing that happened next was the announcement that the clinic was expecting three admissions. Two men and a woman apparently. How old are they? We ask and are told that when we meet them it will be time enough to talk numbers. As usual Rita the oracle filled in some details.

Newbies

Jake – 35-year-old married. Owns a nightclub and drove up in a big flash car, didn't seem ill, or worried about being in rehab – Methamphetamine, - Alcohol, - Anxiety attacks, - Sex addiction.

Vanda – 26-year-old flight attendant. Vanda looked well put together, but needed to retire to her room straight away, pretty sick. – Bulimia - Gambling, - Depression.

Rick – 30s - apparently Rick was a well-known footballer. Looked pretty fit, bronzed and healthy, He was shy however so opted to stay in his room, - Gambling.

The conversation around the meal table was all about the new people, we seemed to be people starved for variety or entertainment and new faces fit the bill. We were informed that none of the newbies were well enough yet to join us, so their stories needed to wait.

Brendon's Story

Brendon said he had grown up in one of the suburbs of Adelaide, he'd had a great family life doing all the things Aussie's are famous for. Surfing and BBQs etc. Two brothers and great parents, nothing out of the ordinary really until senior school. It was around this time that one of his brothers had an accident at work. It was a nasty accident, his brother survived but the aftermath affected everyone in the family in different ways. His mother became very clingy about all her boys, and his father started demanding that he Brendon start working in the family business. Brendon didn't want to and had always said he didn't want to, but after the accident it seemed that life just closed in around everyone and the kids were expected to do what they were told. Brendon said his solution was to leave home and move to Sydney. He started pursuing his love of working around cars, met up with other petrol heads and made a good living. Brendon said he just 'forgot' about home and never talked about his parents or his brothers.

Anyone meeting him at this time would just think he was a loner, just doing his thing around cars. Into this scene strolls Pattie, and she, and Brendon hook up. Pattie was English and on a tourist visa, she wanted to stay in Oz, so she and Brendon cooked up the idea of getting married. A marriage of convenience really, as neither had any wish to make it real. They made their plans and talked about how this was the best solution. They rehearsed all the immigration questions they thought they needed to get right, and without too many difficulties made it possible for Pattie to get her visa to stay in Australia. Probs wouldn't be able to do it these days as things had tightened up so much immigration-wise. I don't know how we got away with it anyhow, but we did. The plan was for them to get divorced at some later date. But in the meantime they would just go on living life in Sydney. They both loved the music scene and nightlife which was always pretty amazing, both had a love of partying and both took copious amounts of anything that was on offer, mostly alcohol and cocaine. Pattie was a lightweight when it came to this type of partying and lifestyle and she got quite sick, quite quickly, their relationship deteriorated with daily arguments. They couldn't see eye to eye about anything anymore. Pattie was angling for more freedom, with Brendon feeling that now they were married it should be different. One day she just up and left and went back to England. He found out when she left that she had also been screwing around with some of their 'so-called friends'. Brendon wasn't certain about that he said, it was just what some had said to him when she left. That was never in the plan, he said, so he followed her back to England to confront her and get divorced.

It was a bloody stupid getting married, for the wrong reasons, but I think we were both nuts at the time. He said his own using continued to get worse and worse, and he could feel his mind slipping away, plus he said I was just so angry at being duped by Pattie. So rehab was the best thing I could think of to do in cold old England. I still haven't found Pattie, but I need to get clean before I can sort this mess out.

"Well done Brendon," says Wolfie, "that was another good attempt to tell us where your addiction took you, but all you've done really is to increase your air of mystery. Scant info on parents or family and on a mission to find your missing wife, who you really shouldn't have married. You can take the words 'think you were nuts' out of the equation, you were most definitely in the realms of insanity to do something so deceptive and possibly illegal.

It feels like you are stranded somewhere in time, and probably need to delve more into your addiction story for us to really get to know you. I also think said Wolfie that there is something else going on with you and Pattie, you could have annulled your marriage from Australia, there was no need really to follow her to England."

"I guess so," said Brendon, no hissy fit from him like Hamish. "To be honest I'm a pretty private person and don't like talking about myself too much. Pattie had been the only person I had let in, and she let me down big time. I felt she ripped my heart out when she left like she did. I still love her and wanted to see if I could rescue this relationship, or at least get an explanation about why she acted like she did, when I had given her everything, even a bloody marriage. I don't want to give up on her or us just yet."

I felt an incredible sadness as Brendon opened up his heart and told us these facts and looking at the faces of everyone in group I suspect we all felt the same. We had all grown quite fond of this blunt Aussie man with a heart of gold.

"You have had a tough time there is no doubt, however in

rehab and in order to find recovery you are going to have to look at what part you played in the things that happened in the story of your life, we will all support you and if you decide you want to find Pattie, we, the clinic will help in any way we can."

"Wow," says I, "none of us really have conventional lives when you dig into them, is that a trait too? I wonder."

"I know a lot of addicts," says Wolfie, "who shun a 'normal' type of lifestyle, and the disease seems to create mayhem and chaos as a matter of course, so things that could be 'normal' always end up as far away from normal as can be."

"On that note we should thank Brendon for his story and take a break from group. Go and get some fresh air, have your comfort breaks etc, as we have more work to do today." We all troop out obediently, some for a cigarette, some for coffee and a chat about the story we had just been part of.

Hamish

There's a bit of a buzz around the place as we hear and then see Hamish arriving back with his suitcases. He comes out of his room and comes to find us, which is new, he never did that before. We all seemed to have 'raised eyebrows' I understand by this what those eyebrow things mean!

"I've come to say I'm sorry," says Hamish, "for my behaviour and for walking out of treatment. Wolfie and the powers that be have been generous in letting me back, but one of the stipulations was that I had to apologise to all of you."

"What did you do, where did you stay? We heard your wife would not let you back home," blurts out Megan. I remember her comments about feeling creeped out by Hamish.

"Quite right too, I've been a bloody idiot, thinking I could fool this place, all of you, as well as thinking my wife would just go along with my lies. She was serious when she told me rehab or nothing. I thought I could convince everyone that I didn't really have a problem, or that the problem was not so bad it needed rehab. The truth is my problems are much worse. I am being investigated by the powers that be, for 'inappropriate behaviour' around my students."

"Oh God not another pervy old man," says Megan, "I thought you said you had retired?"

"Shush child," says Hamish, "it is nothing sexual, but is serious. I have been doing some lecturing at University once a month, my drinking had not been as well hidden as I thought and several of my students wrote a letter telling the Principal I had been drunk on two occasions whilst giving lectures. I don't remember, so have no defence for this. So this and the car crash are hanging over my head."

Hamish is shaking and very contrite as he continues with his sad tale. "When I left treatment the level of drinking increased and I couldn't stop, so in the end even I was sick of myself and begged the clinic to let me back."

"Oh mate," said Aiden, "you did the right thing in coming back, you will be more able to sort out all of the things you talked about if you are sober, if you continue to drink it will all just get worse. We have been taught that this disease is progressive and unless we stop it in its tracks by practicing abstinence it just gets worse, and by looking at you old man this is so true."

"I know," says Hamish looking quite deflated as well as shaky and sick," I thought I was going to be ok, I hadn't drunk in 2 weeks and felt great so thought I was cured, you know the exception to everyone else. But hell, as soon as I was free of this place and my wife refused to let me home, the rage I have inside of me boiled over and taking a drink was the only way to stop it. Then once I started I couldn't stop. It's ten times worse after a period of sobriety."

"I think people call that being dry drunk," says Rita whose been standing on the side-lines listening, "unless you do some work on yourself all the traits we all have, remain and continue to plague us. Without drinking and/or without the programme we find the world and ourselves much too difficult. Remember our addiction is a solution to our woes, that's why we do it. None of us are stupid, but we all find life on life's terms difficult to deal with."

"I'm pretty impressed with the therapy team," says I. "How is it they always seem to know more about us then we are willing to talk about?"

"I told you Wolfie always hits the target," said Brendon, "the team are a bit magic to be honest, bloody bastards at times, but they know me better than I know myself."

"Or maybe there's a 'mole' in the place," says Pavla. "You know a spy who runs back and tells the staff everything."

With her accent this statement sounded even more nuts.

"Who would you imagine that could be? A bit paranoid don't you think," replies Brendon, "whose got the time or inclination for that bullshit?"

"Just saying," says Pavla.

We all agree however that the therapy team are a bit like magic in everything they can see without us telling them.

WORKSHOP
SABOTAGING YOUR TREATMENT/RECOVERY

Statistics about Recovery are rarely collated or published. The reason?

They are extremely difficult to collect. People who relapse don't want to be contacted.

It is fair to say that many more people relapse than remain clean and sober.

Relapse IS NOT Inevitable. However sabotage is always present in Relapses.

WHAT IS SABOTAGE?

Wilful destruction, Deliberate, Undermining. (Note act of the Will)

HOW DO WE SABOTAGE?

Not paying attention to feelings. Not going to meetings or working the programme.

Ignoring stress, or anxiety, or anger, or shame, or sadness. Not being honest.

Ignoring H.A.L.T. Hunger, Anger, Loneliness or Tiredness.

Denial, 'there's nothing wrong, I don't need to talk about…'

Isolation, which develops from those adverse feelings

and the above thought process.

Going to 'Risky' places and mixing with 'Risky' people, doing 'Risky' things.

If you don't know what 'Risky' is, find out before it is too late.

Thinking 'I know what's best for me' – Not sharing – Blaming others.

Dishonesty in all its forms. 95% honesty does not work!

I want to use, = I want to change these feelings, – and doing nothing about it.

10: The New Gang in Town

The three new people were in fairly good shape compared to what some of us had looked like when we arrived. They came to join us in the lounge room as we were winding down for the day, the talk was small and inconsequential for a bit as everyone sussed each other out.

Malc the night nurse came to sit with us, and the discussion got a bit more personal and deeper. We told the three what to expect over the next few days, keeping it fairly light. Some comparisons of substances and lifestyles were being made but nothing too drastic was being discussed. Vanda and Rick were the first to fold and said they were exhausted and needed to rest. Jake stayed and when we questioned him he seemed pretty open.

Jake

Jake began to talk and pretty soon we were all involved in his story, we didn't usually chat openly like this in the lounge room at night we tended to keep our revelations for the therapy team, but Jake obviously needed to talk and none of us wanted to shut him down. Including Malc the nurse. We figured if Malc was ok with it then so were we, and Malc would hand it over to the therapists tomorrow.

I'm 35 and own a nightclub with my husband Graham, said Jake, there I've got that out of the way he said, I always feel I have to get that said to gauge the lie of the land, are you friendly or shocked or unconcerned. I've had such problems with all sorts about my being gay, the worst being my parents. My mother just ignores it, as though it is a problem to be ignored and Dad doesn't acknowledge Graham, or our life together. It's pretty terrible really. Let alone what happened in school, makes me shudder.

"I think you will find us all quite open-minded," says Malc.

Jake gives a small smile and continues with his description of his life.

Our business is pretty good but the lifestyle that goes with it includes copious amounts of drugs. Even though I have wanted to stop for the longest time I haven't been able to. My relationship with Graham is suffering and to be honest I'm here to try to save it, and probably our business too. My using has really spiked in the last few months and I can't seem to stop. I'm doing and saying ridiculous and sometimes dangerous things. Graham and I are arguing a lot, we used to be exclusive but recently we both have had affairs. Our business is suffering, we used to have the best nightclub on the South Coast, but with my attention distracted I have let the standards slip, and way too much trouble is finding its way through the doors. There's much more to this of course but I've only just met you and perhaps need to keep some of it for the therapy?

"Well done for being as open as you have been," says Malc, "that was brave, but you are going to learn pretty quickly that if we are not doing this for ourselves it probably won't work, but you've got time to work on all of that. For now though welcome to this very exclusive club!"

"Ourselves?" Says Jake," are you telling me, that you're an addict too?"

" Yes," Malc said, "I'm a nurse here but also a recovering addict with several years of clean time. Most of the staff here are recovering addicts, so you're in good company!"

"That actually makes me feel better, looking at you I would never have known," says Jake.

"I don't think you could actually tell with most of us, Aiden chips in, none of us 'look' particularly ill, maybe some of us when we were in detox perhaps, but not generally."

"None of us are low-bottom users or drunks," says Brendon.

"That sounds terrible," says Molly, "but I know what you mean, the lecture on the Disease Concept explained all about this being a progressive disease and with the advances in treatment none of us have had to end up in an alley with a needle or booze in a paper bag."

We suddenly all remember Pete and tell Jake about this 30-year-old man who died from addiction and hypothermia. The room goes silent in memory of the man.

Malc says "that just goes to highlight that this is not just a disease of the body, but also of the mind and the spirit, if our minds are so affected by our addictions we can lose the will to live. Any of you who are suffering with a dual diagnosis such as Depression or Anxiety will have felt some of the depths that Pete sank to when he tried to get clean. That bit is always sad, some people just don't make it. Pete couldn't face confronting the abyss."

"Yeah that's what it feels like sometimes, says Brendon, a bloody scary black mass where a life should be, it isn't easy to do this Rehab thing, but you Malc and people like the therapy team and some of the ex-peers from this place all give us hope that it is possible to change and recover."

"Well thank you," said Malc, "we like to hear that we make a difference. Some of you have heard the workshop on suicide, so know that this population, the population of alcoholism and other addictions are up there in the high echelons of death by suicide. Pete's death will most likely be recorded as death by hypothermia. Alcoholism or addiction may not get a mention. I would say many deaths by addiction don't get recorded as such. There are other ways to die from this disease of course. A whole plethora of health woes, accidents, and violence. This is really not a pretty world, yet it has, especially in the realm of parties and 'good times' the reputation of being both glamorous and fun."

"The fun stuff for all of us had deserted us a long time ago or was so minimal it really didn't make much sense to continue to search for the highs," said Brendon. "But we could not get off the merry go round no matter how hard we wanted to."

"Well," said Malc, "hopefully all of you will find the answers here. The road to recovery is not easy but is most definitely worthwhile. You have to find out what needs to change, then be willing to do the work to make change possible, and then, to continue to do it. This is not a one-time thing, or a 'one thing fits everyone' kind of solution. It's individualised and sometimes quite hard or complicated. It all depends on the lives you've lived and how far your disease has progressed."

"Not easy then," said Jake, "and there I was thinking all I had to do was come into this place, you would help me stop using and show me how to control it all."

We all laughed and nodded in recognition.

"Ok everyone, I think enough is enough, remember Jake is a newcomer he needs to ease in gently and the rest of you have a busy day of therapy again tomorrow, and for some of you it will be your first trip out to Narcotics Anonymous and Alcoholics Anonymous this weekend, so you need to rest up in preparation."

"Oh God," says Megan "do I have to go?"

"Yeah you do," said Malc, "we will ask the therapy team to give the group some time tomorrow to discuss why the meetings are important, but remember like everything else, in the end you are the one that decides what you will do or not do in pursuit of Recovery. In rehab, you do HAVE to go, but once you leave MF it is your choice. If your thinking hasn't changed by then, you are destined to go round in ever-decreasing circles."

On that note we trooped out to get rested for the day tomorrow and my thoughts turned to outside meetings, and like Megan had an internal strop of 'Do I really need to do this bloody meeting thing?'

The meetings, however, were the least of my worries just now. The whole business about the car and my killing someone was driving me nuts. Secrets were definitely keeping me sick, and I couldn't seem to concentrate with the worry of it all in my head. I knew I would have to get honest if I wanted to make any progress with recovery. I had decided I wanted recovery but was frightened at what it might cost me.

I made a bargain with myself that I would go to one of the staff soon and confess. Even if I went to jail it might be better than this worry that was making me crazy.

11: Bloody Meetings and Megan's story

We've been in group saying hi to the newcomers and discussing clinic business and also the topics of last night.

Megan will tell her story a bit later, but I think we need to discuss meetings outside of the clinic and why we think they are important.

Sindy and Laura are taking group today and as they both go to meetings I presume they are best placed in discussing this topic.

Meetings

What are they, why are they, and do we have to go?

The Anonymous movement began in Britain in the 1950s, after having a launch in America in the '30s. Before this, the fate of most addicts, be it alcoholism or any other drug was pretty dire. We ended up in prison, in mental institutions, and not nice ones like MF but real straight jacket type places, or on the street. No-one knew what to do with addicts whose illness had progressed to the serious problems stage. The behaviour looked like insanity, so mental institutions fit the story, or were illegal so fit being

locked up. The street addicts were to be avoided at all costs.

Two alcoholic men met, and in that meeting the cosmos shifted. They were first of all able to stay clean and sober, they had each tried many ways and been unable to succeed before this meeting. It was this, and the fact both men were pretty smart cookies, a GP and a Businessman, they devised the method that is known as Alcoholics Anonymous today. It started with those two, grew to a hundred people, they then wrote a book about it and today it is a worldwide organisation. The story of it all is pretty spectacular when you understand the odds of it happening in the first place. The meetings are the place where the methods devised by those two men are talked about. Today there are many different branches of the same organisation, so as well as AA you have, Cocaine Anonymous and Narcotics Anonymous, and Gamblers Anonymous and so on, the same philosophy underpins all the groups, but the name of the preferred substance or behaviour is different. Amazing when you think there are no moneymen behind it all, no sponsorship, just word of mouth.

Everyone thinks its religious, and for some it is, but mainly it is a philosophy that enables the person seeking answers to problems created by addiction to find them, mainly by talking and listening to other people with the same issues. It all sounds pretty farfetched when we try to describe what goes on, but it works. We are sober!

I think to begin with everyone has issues with the organisation, it has not got a 'sexy' reputation, it is old school and let's not forget why people seek it out. They are usually in dire straits and the trouble and hopelessness that attaches itself to the illness of addiction almost overtakes anything else that occurs around it.

We at the clinic, teach you that abstinence is one of the cornerstones to anything that can occur in recovery. When abstinence is accepted, healing and recovery can begin, but that is not all that needs to occur in the programme of recovery. It seems that we addicts have short memory spans, our thinking is pretty flawed, we have really twisted wires, so we can lose focus on the need for abstinence very quickly. The Anonymous meetings serve as a reminder to this. The people attending are like-minded individuals, so in a meeting we find people who understand and can help keep us on the straight and narrow. The 'steps' which are spoken about at the meetings, are a systemised way of working on problems, resolving them and ensuring we stay well. It's not rocket science of course, but it is vital that we learn how important on-going focus is. The relapse rates are sadly very high, as people do not stick around long enough to hear or understand the message of

recovery. Lots of myths and misconceptions in this organisation, and the bizarre twisted thinking in addictions are all reasons why so many people fail or misunderstand this way of recovering. If you only stay your allotted time at the Clinic there is no chance you will stay in recovery. There is way too much to learn and understand. Change is hard, and none of you know what needs to change yet. It is doubtful you will learn all you need by the end of your time at Moriatta Falls, what you will have is a good start. But that is all it is, a start.

"Phew!" Says the therapist "enough of my voice now, I'm hoping you have questions about this?"

"Yeah," says Megan, "do we HAVE to go?"

Ignoring some of the groans from some of the group, Lorna very patiently reiterates some of the facts, and adds: "We introduce you to the meetings, take you to them as a group to cut some of the fear factor. Our hopes are that you will see their value when you get to know some of the people who go to them. If you choose not to attend when you leave treatment, it is doubtful you will remain clean and sober. But while you are in treatment, yes, you have to go."

"Ok group, it seems appropriate if we move straight onto Megan's story, and maybe she will answer her own question about the need to go to meetings."

Megan

I live at home with my mother and father, they are pretty cool parents and have always given me lots of freedom. I loved school and have always been encouraged by them to explore and question, so I developed a love of learning pretty early on. I got bullied a bit for being a geek, but my big brother is a musician, which helped make me seem a bit cooler. I am so proud of him, we all are. It is partly in hopes of measuring up to him that I pushed myself so hard at school and now at University, but all that happened was I got super stressed and anxious about exams.

One of my friends introduced me to cannabis when I was at school and I loved this as it chilled me right out. At University the drugs doing the circuit were of the cocaine or crack variety which I would not touch in a month of Sunday's, I hate alcohol as I have seen how stupid people get on it. Ketamine was introduced to me by my ex-boyfriend last year. This drug has a big rep as a very quick way to de-stress, so I was pretty keen to try it. My mood was getting pretty low and I found I wasn't able to study or concentrate. At first Ketamine was the answer, it was perfect, but then as I got used to it, I needed more to get the effect I wanted until things started to spiral out of control. I was taking loads of both drugs and nothing was actually working any more. I was getting more and more stressed. I had to drop out of my studies, luckily my exams have been deferred as I had been talking to the campus therapy team. In the end, it was they who recommended a deferment and treatment before I returned to my studies. To be honest I was one of those people we talked about in the Suicide workshop. I was pretty low, crying all day, not eating and sometimes self-harming. Megan then showed us her arms which were full of burn marks and scars where she had gouged herself.

My parents were shocked to say the least, they had no idea I was feeling so low, they acted immediately and got me an admission to MF.

"Well done Megan," we all say.

"Didn't realise you were so low kid, or that you had self-harmed, you are still quite secretive and still hide things really well (or really badly)," says Aiden.

The therapist led the congratulations and feedback, then asked Megan if she could be convinced that meetings, especially after discharge from treatment, could be a way of keeping her mood stable. Her self-harming was being managed with help from the staff and prescription medication, and since her admission to the clinic she had not felt the need to actually burn or cut herself.

"I do have issues with the meetings," said Megan, everyone seems so old. It feels like a cult and people do talk about God and stuff, but I will give it a go if you say I have to. I don't know if I will ever like them, but I do know I feel better today. I don't want to go back to hating myself and my life. My arms are disgusting, and I can never wear short sleeves, I don't really want people to see or know. The urge to do it gets so strong some times. Its stronger than the urge to use drugs to be honest. But using drugs takes away the urge to self-harm. I have been able to manage all my urges by talking to staff, and the docs gave me some medication to help with my anxiety. I feel like a new person at the moment."

"Oh you poor little thing, but I think you've hit the target Megan," says Rita, "my desire to stay well far outweighs my prejudice about the meetings. I plan to go for about six months in the hope I like them in the end. If after six months I still hate them I will re-think my strategy and options. If the meetings help stop the self- harm or our desire to use, surly it's worth giving them a try?"

"That's a brilliant idea," says Megan, "can I adopt your plan too? Do you think it a good plan Laura and Sindy?"

They both smiled and said it was a perfect plan.

I wish my problems could be so easily solved I thought.

"What sup Blue," said Brendon," I can see you looking more and more distracted, come on give it up, tell me what's wrong. Nothing changes if nothing changes as they say."

"If I tell you something about me will you keep it to yourself?" I ask.

"Of course, I'm the best secret-keeper in the world."

We go into the garden and find a quiet place, before I know it everything comes tumbling out, the blackout, the drive here, the dents in the car and the blood I found in the dents. My worry, my sleeplessness, and fear I'll be put in prison.

Brendon looks suitably serious. "Are you sure it was blood he says?"

I told him about the credit cards and running my hand over the dents.

"So you are not entirely sure?"

"Well I am sure about the dents and am almost sure I found blood. I keep expecting the police to come and get me but nothing yet."

"We have to go and have a look," says Brendon.

"But we can't say I." "The car is in the car park, and we are not allowed out there without an escort."

"You know Mimi if we all did what we were allowed to do all of the time, none of us would be here, we are going to bend the rules just this once in order for you to be able to sleep at night."

With that he got up and climbed the garden fence into the car park. He opened the gate which had a bolt on the other side and let me out.

With me feeling like a criminal, we snuck into the car park, found my car and studied the dents and scratches.

"Well you've certainly done some damage Blue, but where's the blood?"

I whispered, "well there was hardly any when I first found it, maybe it's been washed away."

"There has been no rain in the last week's, so nothing has washed away as you say. But look!"

He points at a red streak. "That's not blood, its red berries. You idiot you've obviously driven through some heavy shrubbery and collected red berries along the way."

My body went hot and cold and I suddenly wanted to faint. Brendon laughed at my reaction, which made me stiffen with indignation.

"Don't laugh at me I thought I'd killed someone." I laughed as I said it, with relief and with pure joy at the realisation I had not become a murderer. I had been worried for nothing. Well not nothing but certainly not murder.

We retraced our steps pledging allegiance to each other for breaking the rules. I felt so happy I gave Brendon a huge hug. Holding him tight and thanking him with everything I had in me.

"Whoa, there sweetheart! Stop all of this or they'll be thinking things about us next."

"Oh Brendon, I am just so grateful, I have been worried about this for so long now, I've hardly slept. Thanks for breaking the rules and for helping me, if ever you need anything, I'm your girl, just ask."

With that I left him and cried all the way back to my room,

avoiding bumping into anyone, which might have needed an explanation.

I got back to my room and sank to the ground in the universal position for prayers, never being very religious but feeling my thanks to the universe for saving me from murder and prison needed a gesture of sorts.

"To whatever," I began, "from the bottom of my heart, I am giving thanks. I promise with everything I can promise I will stay clean and sober and never have to be in such a position again."

I'd made countless promises never to drink or use again before coming here, but the realisation of what might have happened really sunk in, and I vowed I would never let it happen again. I would do this bloody recovery whatever it might cost in time money or anything else.

12: Aftercare Meeting at Moriatta Falls/Relapse

In order to create the strongest recovery possible I need to agree to some basic principles and rules. In signing this agreement I hereby give my group and therapists at MF permission to assess and question me about my behaviour. I also consent to the following:

- Honesty and Confidentiality are strict requirements of attendance at Aftercare.
- Relapses cannot be kept secret; I will talk to staff at MF about my own or others relapses.
- I will agree not to come back to the clinic unless I am at least 28 days clean and sober.
- I will attend at least 3 Fellowship meetings weekly.
- I will avoid risky places and risky people especially in the first months after discharge.
- I will inform my family and the people I mix with about my new rules.
- I will ask family and friends not to drink or drug around me.

- **I will avoid holidays for the first 6 months of my recovery.**
- **I will keep my home alcohol and drug free, allowing it to become my 'safe haven'.**
- **I will avoid new romantic liaisons, and work on my current relationships.**
- **I will ask for help from my group and the staff at Moriatta Falls.**

My first experience of Aftercare was that I hated it.

Bloody interlopers, I thought, interfering with my peace and quiet. Who the hell were they kidding with their smiles and happy talk?

I managed the first half of the meeting when the rules and regulations were discussed but then legged it, going to find a member of staff and opting out of the remainder of the afternoon feigning a headache.

The next day when we processed the previous day and the meeting in particular, I was able to be honest about my feelings, expecting to get shot down in flames. Surprisingly though everyone including the therapists seemed to understand my thinking and sympathised with it. I was told my tolerance levels would improve in time and hopefully I would discover that this meeting in particular was a huge resource in my on-going quest to stay well in recovery.

Megan then pipes up with some questions that I must

admit were running through my head. "Are you telling me she said that all those people agree to not mix with using people anymore? That they won't get into relationships and will go to meetings?"

Wolfie responds with, "you know Megan, the reality about addictions is that more people relapse than ever stay well, the relapse rates are appalling, the Aftercare regulars have come up with some of the agreements in order to try to address these statistics. Most of the people at the meeting are sticking to the 'rules' for now because they are convinced it works for them. Each of the people you met yesterday have seen their share of people who continue to break rules and who suffer the consequences. There are many more people who attend Aftercare, they don't all come regularly, but they all stay in touch with MF via email or the phone. In this way we can gauge that the people we hear from are sticking to the 'rules' and are today clean and sober. Our success rates are quite impressive." He paused for breath.

"These things that we ask you to do seem prescriptive and in some way they are, but each of the rules is there to keep you safe. Change is the hardest thing to achieve, and some of these boundaries and rules are what make change possible. The agreement simply asks you to do some of these things for a period of six months. It is thought that this will give you time to adjust and become used to a different way of living. All of the things you are agreeing not to do are high risk things. Things that create stress. In the end when your recovery is solid, you can actually do anything and everything you want except use. In the beginning though you don't even know what you want to do."

"Yes," says Rita "we hear about listening to or sticking with the 'winners' the winners in my book are the people keeping clean and sober. It all makes sense."

"So what happens if someone relapses? Surely coming back to the clinic at a time like this is necessary, like me?" says Hamish.

Wolfie says, "of course it is important, however we cannot allow people who are in relapse to mix with the in-patient population. In a sense you in-patient are the more important people in the building. Also the most fragile. You came back into treatment Hamish so are allowed to go to Aftercare, if you hadn't come back into treatment you would not be allowed back to Aftercare until you were at least a month clean again. Relapse is very destructive, and Aftercare is not the place it can be dealt with. We never just turn people away; we want to know what's going on and will do everything we can to help. But if you relapse after treatment, you must either come back into treatment, or try to get clean using the outside meetings. There is no one thing fits all." He continues with:

"When we talk to people who have relapsed we can generally discover things they have either been doing or failed to do to answer why the relapse occurred. We have pieces of work called a Relapse Analysis which looks at and tries to work out what has been going on. There have been many fine therapy teams over the years who have looked at relapse, there is a great deal that has been written about the subject. It seems to be a common part of some peoples recovery, but it is not inevitable. What you do will dictate your success or otherwise in this area, and what you do or don't do is paramount."

Some of the questions you need to answer about your relapse are:

Do you believe addiction is an illness that requires abstinence?

What were your thoughts leading up to the using behaviour? What feelings did you have just before picking up. What excuse did you give yourself for using again?

Have you been attending meetings? Did you find a sponsor? Did you engage in work on the steps? – Or how did you look after your Mental Health?

What happened as you began using, tell the story. Who or what were you blaming for your actions, or how did you justify your actions?

Did you endanger yourself or others, did you break the law? How?

Who else has been affected by your behaviour?

How do you feel about your actions?

Have you learnt anything and what are you going to do next?

Wolfie also explains that a relapse can only occur after a period of sobriety or clean time when you have been working a programme. **So before Moriatta Falls even though some of you only binge used, the periods in-between were not classed as recovery but simply as a period of not using. Sometimes also called 'dry drunk'. The feelings, behaviours and attitudes that accompany the disease all remain present and active. The 'using' is actually only a small part of the problem. The rest of it is 'why' we use. Addicts have to be abstinent of course, but there is so much more that needs to happen.**

There are many things an individual will need to recommence doing if they are to stay clean and abstinence and going to meetings is most definitely up there as one of the most important. Rehab in a sense is the training ground for how to stay clean and sober. It is here you learn how to talk and connect with others. Recovering people have to understand very early on that communication and connection are essential components in the job of staying clean. Addicts are good at isolating and keeping secrets, these things enable the illness to grow.

There are a few other things about relapse that you need to know:

Post-Acute Withdrawal Syndrome or PAWS

Withdrawal symptoms are well recognised and are pretty awful, some are more distressing than others, but are a part of getting clean. What most people don't realise however is that symptoms can re-occur for up to two years after the first withdrawal from your drugs or behaviours of abuse. These second-stage withdrawals are mainly psychological and emotional rather than physical. They occur as your brain chemistry and functions attempt to return to normal. As the brain improves the levels in brain chemistry fluctuate which creates PAWS. Some of the symptoms can be mood swings, irritability, depression, tiredness or variable energy levels, disturbed sleep and variable concentration and motivation. They are changeable and come and go. Not everyone experiences all of them but when you do, they feel bad and can lead to more feelings of 'is this worth it?' You need to know they will improve again. It is your body trying to heal, the best way of dealing with them is to communicate, step up your recovery plans and stay abstinent. They can last from a few hours or a few days and there are no obvious triggers. You could also learn to be kind to yourself by investing in yoga and meditation classes, maybe some massage or acupuncture. Any and many things to calm and treat your body and mind with respect. Most addicts have learnt to isolate and hide away especially in times of stress, this is the worst thing you can do. You have to remember that you alone cannot heal yourselves, you need help.

There are three distinct stages to a relapse:

<u>Emotional.</u> Your emotions are in a state of heightened anxiety or stress. You may be very defensive or have mood swings. You become discontent and unhappy with everything you are doing. Recovery is not giving you what you want, it's boring and dull as you are moving into the <u>Mental phase</u>. Perhaps the cravings have returned at this stage. There is usually an internal fight going on, very secretive of course, about staying clean, which in the end the addiction will win. Remember you are powerless over the disease. You cannot and will not win in any negotiation with it. <u>The physical stage</u> of course is to use. The battle will be lost, and insanity has returned. The insanity of course begins long before the using starts. It begins as soon as the discontent and/or unhappy feelings return, and you do nothing about them.

13: Pretty Names, Ugly Behaviours

Jake, Vanda and Rick have all joined us for these discussions in group. We had learnt a lot about Jake the night he joined us in the TV room, but now much to their bemusement they are all invited to tell the group about themselves. Jake offers to continue his story from the previous night. Vanda and Rick breathe sighs of relief.

Jake

Jake said, well the only thing I want to add to my sorry tale of why I am here is that my husband Graham and I were involved in something called Chem Sex. Which is where we joined other people to experiment with sex and used a cocktail of chemicals to add to the excitement of it all. We were heavily into methamphetamine which we called Tina, such a pretty name for a very ugly drug says Jake. Some alcohol joined the party as well as Viagra to 'force' the high into a different stratosphere. Like I said, we used to be exclusive, but things spiralled very out of control, very quickly, both in terms of the risks we were taking in having sex with strangers but also in the cocktails of drugs we were taking, and how we were taking them. The drugs were the first thing to be used, which increased the excitement of what was to come next, once the party started we could text out to others in our scene to come and join the party. We had multiple acts with multiple partners.

It was sordid and vile, but oh so exciting. When an event ended, and reality came calling I was always sick and shaky, sweating buckets and unable to see straight let alone go to work and concentrate on what I had to do there. I was often paranoid that other straight people would know what I had been up to. Shamed even though I couldn't wait for it all to happen again. I craved the excitement of it all despite it making me sick and paranoid. The obsession never ended. Whatever happened or how many people I had sex with I was never satisfied. Showering couldn't make me feel clean or stop the sweating, but I couldn't resist wanting it again. You know the 'parties' were much worse than I am telling you now, I will tell you on a one to one Wolfie as my therapist but feel I most likely have said more than enough right now, about the scene.

Graham and I both knew we were engaged in very risky behaviour, Graham pulled out of this sordid game much quicker than I did, and our relationship is hanging by a thread. I haven't been able to stop which is why I am here. I feel sick to my stomach at the crazy lifestyle I have allowed to develop around Graham and myself. I may have destroyed my marriage, and my health is pretty poor. I have no excuse; I have a great job. Things used to be amazing with Graham, yet this need for excitement is stronger than anything he might mean to me. I am being so open about it all because I'm desperate to stop and desperate to save my marriage. You know there is no glamour any more, if there ever was in any of my story, it's all cold and functional. The only high I get is in the preparation for it all. The buzz of expectation, which goes really quick. It's just sad. I'm just sad. But I can't seem to stop the behaviour, I'm hooked into it and the need for it all is stronger than my need to stop at the moment. I so hope coming here can help?

"Phew," said Wolfie, "that was very courageous Jake, well done, with that kind of honesty you deserve to make it. We don't know yet if your marriage can be saved, or if your health can be restored. What we can ensure though is that you receive the best treatment for your addictions which are behavioural as well as chemical. Your behaviour sounds like sex-addiction, as well as substance abuse. Being cross-addicted always adds to the difficulties in getting and staying sober. It won't be easy, but we can help stop this spiral downwards if you work with us. Some of the medications we can give you will help with the cravings, and as you learn to talk more and develop more coping strategies things may improve for you. But it's going to be a tough road my friend."

Jake nodded, looking a bit sick as he accepted our congratulations and encouragement." I don't feel like I should be congratulated about any of this ugliness," he said.

"Ok," says Wolfie, "Mimi, Vanda and Rick, we will hear your histories later in the week, let's break for today. The congratulations Jake are in honour of your bravery in opening up, everyone in this room knows how hard that is."

"Remember everyone, the law for rules of engagement,"

WHAT IS SAID IN THIS ROOM STAYS IN THIS ROOM

Confidentiality is one of the cornerstones of the programme.

Jake looks relieved to hear this being said. Vanda Rick and I all say we feel scared at having to speak, all of us say we are willing to do so. How can we not after Jake. He goes to talk to the therapy team.

Our working day is over, we scatter, some for cigarettes, some for coffee, some for solitude.

Insanity

Oh God, the feeling in me is sad, sad, sad, sad. I feel sick again. My head is banging, and a familiar feeling starts to envelop me. I am feeling dizzy and disorientated. I need help but choose solitude. I heard what Jake did and it terrifies me, I can't be like him, I can't do this.

I scuttle back to the safety of my room. I'm inspired by others' bravery, but it doesn't make me any braver. I know

I promised the universe I would do anything for sobriety, but this is just too much. That shitty story has frightened me. I'm gonna leave. They can all just tell their stupid stories; I'm not going to.

This feeling I feel right now has followed me all my life. It's got me by the throat now, it won't let go, I feel I can't breathe, I can't see or hear or move very well. I'm disappearing.

I learnt how to cope with this and make myself invisible from a very young age. Most people don't know what I mean by 'disappearing', but anyone growing up in an alcoholic home will know. It seems some of this new group I find myself in could also know.

Being invisible means you don't get singled out; you don't get into any trouble. You stay invisible for as long as you can, silent so he doesn't take any notice of you, quiet so he can't be distracted by you. He rants and he raves but misses you by a mile.

It's a skill I developed from a very early age, and it worked well when I was little. He never did single me out or notice me. It worked because I escaped his alcoholic wrath, I tried to teach it to my siblings, but they didn't want to be invisible, they fought back or joined in the arguments, or ran away from home and got into trouble with the law. My brother was a wildling and drove motorbikes so fast we thought he would fly. His rage at our father was fierce and he never learned how to combat it because he crashed on his bike one crazy rainy day. He crashed and broke my heart when he left me.

I was the invisible child, the good girl, I stayed out of trouble, I stayed alive and disappeared almost completely into addiction.

My eyes started streaming as all these memories smashed uninvited into my senses. The clamour in my head was epic, so loud it hurt. It didn't matter because I don't want to think, I don't want to remember. The craving started then as it always did. If ever I wanted a drink or drug, it was now, the craving was so strong I thought I might scream. It was growing and black, it was shutting out all light and awareness. I knew what would help me, it always did, I need it, I want it. This place can go to hell, they can all go to hell.

I start pacing round and round in my room, I was panting like a wild animal, hitting my head and moaning. I can't breathe, I can't think. I'm trying to work out how to leave, what to do next. I thought it was all just silent inside me as usual, but I must have been making a noise as Nurse May and Malc came into my room.

They held me as my body shook and the tears and shaking overwhelmed me, they stayed with me and made comforting gestures in an effort to calm me down. Rubbing my back, stroking my hands, telling me it was going to be all right.

"It won't ever be all right," I shouted at them, "it can

never be all right." I pushed them away and swore at them. "Fuck off and leave me alone, I don't need you, I'm going to leave, fuck off. That bastard won, he made us all into what we are, and I will never forgive him. My brother is dead, DEAD! I screamed don't you understand? It will never be alright."

I began pulling clothes out of the drawers and cupboards, "leave me alone, leave me alone." My fury at the world came spewing out of my mouth aimed at these two who were trying to help.

In a repeat of what had happened on my first night in this place, Nurse May was wiping my face with a damp cloth. Whilst Malc left the room to fetch some medication.

After what seemed to be a very long time, I had no tears left to cry. Malc had returned with water and some medication which he made me take. Eventually my shaking stopped, and I was able to hear what May and Malc were saying to me.

They continued to talk normally to me, no recrimination in their voices, no reprimand, nothing but kindness and understanding. They encouraged me to lie down on my bed and pulled the covers over me to keep me warm. The blackness began to dissolve, my shaking stopped and the noise in my head calmed down.

"Well there you go Mimi," said May," I guess your days of hiding are over. All of that stuff you've just cried out has been waiting to spill ever since you arrived. If you run away now, or go back to hiding in your silence, you will never be free my love. You've started to talk so you really should continue tomorrow when Wolfie asks you for your story."

As I listened to their voices, a calmness seemed to wash over me, perhaps the pills had kicked in, but I didn't really care what it was, I was just glad not to have the ball of sorrow, blackness and pain that lived inside of me radiating out anymore. It was subdued for now. Get some sleep Mimi the two nurses said as they left me.

I awoke several hours later, my head hurt a bit and I was dehydrated and very thirsty, but the pain in my chest which had always been there seemed to have gone. The quietness was lovely, peaceful. I looked around my room which I expected to see devastated from my tantrum, but it was tidy and calm, Malc and May must have picked everything up and sorted things out. As I drank some water I could feel it trickle down my throat, it gelt good. It felt real. I felt real and whole, no longer invisible. Maybe I don't need to hide any more I thought as visions of my beautiful brother played through my mind.

He's gone Mimi, he isn't coming back, but destroying yourself because he's gone will do nothing to change his death. I could hear his voice agreeing with me, his smile encouraging me. I started crying again, but these tears were different, I will always miss you my darling. It will never be alright, but I will stop trying to finish what our upbringing had started.

He was in my head as I went back to sleep. No dreams or nightmares this night.

14: Megan, Aiden and the Great Escape

We were all ushered into group the next day, all of the therapy team looking serious and a little bit sick if truth be known.

Oh God now what? I think as I notice Megan and Aiden were absent. I hoped nothing too serious as I was feeling a little fragile after my freak out yesterday. Secretly glad that issues about others meant I would not be the order of the day. – Selfish bitch, I thought. My gratitude to Brendon knew no bounds, I was released from a grisly secret about murder, but it still did not make this 'confession' stuff any easier to do.

"Yet again," said Wolfie, "we have some shocking news."

"Late last night we received a call from Megan's parents saying she had contacted them telling them she had left treatment with her 'boyfriend' It has taken us some time to work out from his absence that they were talking about Aiden."

"Crikey!" says Brendon sounding very Oz-like in this one-word exclamation of shock.

"We have contacted the police and sent them round to the address of the hotel Megan said they were in. From what anyone can gather, Aiden and Megan had decided to run away together last night. No-one saw them leave, and as they are both not on high observation levels they timed their escape in-between checks. They drove to a hotel, scoped out some drugs and alcohol and started to use, according to Megan, Aiden then had a meltdown and would not let her leave the room they were staying in. She was in a bit of a state on the phone to her parents, who are also in a bit of a state talking to us, everyone appears as shocked as you all seem to be. The police are on their way there now and we will let you know what happens. Did anyone realise they were getting close? Staff certainly missed any signs, in fact at times Megan seemed to dislike Aiden."

We were all puzzled more than anything. None of us had an inkling that a romance or 'special friendship' had been building. None of us had any idea an escape plan was forming.

"I thought Aiden had a girlfriend called Naomi," said Rita.

"Naomi has been out of the picture for some time," said Brendon. "They'd been arguing a lot about where to live and about money. She refused to come to the Family Programme and Aiden got really mad at her, and they broke up."

"But Megan for Christ's sake, she's a child," said Hamish.

"Yep there is that," said Wolfie. "But then again she is an adult, 19 is not classed a child. Her parents however are traumatised by events and it will take some sorting out by all concerned."

"What's going to happen?" I asked.

"We don't actually know right now;" said Sindy "we have to wait for the police and to see if either of them will explain their actions. For now, why don't we all have a break?" Sindy continues with, "Jake, Vanda and Rick apologies to you all for this intrusion into what is usually a very safe and respectful place. I can guarantee this is a very rare occurrence, staff can usually spot very quickly if an inappropriate relationship is developing, but this time we did not. We will recommence later and let you all know if we receive any news."

The discussions in the scuzzy smoking area ranged from shock to anger to pity and sadness. Everyone just couldn't believe they could pull off such a thing without any one of us realising or noticing they had anything planned.

"Just shows how manipulative and dishonest we can be, and no wonder addicts have a bad rep, pulling stunts like this. Is it any wonder addicts become misunderstood and rejects of society. If even a rehab can't control our behaviour there doesn't seem to be much hope does there?" These words by Brendon ran in our ears as we retreated into our own thoughts again.

Insanity

The therapy team gathered us all into the lounge room,

saying they wanted it to feel a little bit comforting and less like a group therapy session.

"Megan," Wolfie said, "was currently at home but would be on her way to another rehab in America. She had wanted to return to MF, but the team felt it would be too distracting to the current in-patient group. Her parents thought she would do better somewhere remote to the present circumstances, and they have relatives in America. With our help they have found her a place in another rehab. She had been the one to phone home, by locking herself in the bathroom when Aiden fell asleep. She said that after they began to use, Ketamine Coke and Alcohol all hell broke out between them. Aiden just got more and more crazy, talking about being God and being able to fix everyone. Megan grew increasingly terrified and begged to be let out of the room, he wouldn't let her go and so she had to wait until he fell asleep, and then to give her credit acted quite rationally by contacting her parents."

Sindy added "they had been getting close for a little while and had talked about meeting up after rehab, but after our discussion in group about having to go to meetings Megan had said they should leave immediately. She didn't want to face going to meetings. She said they both didn't like some of the rules and regulations of rehab but also of the Aftercare agreement."

Wolfie carries on with, "Aiden has been less talkative to staff and the police; he has actually been sectioned and is in a hospital having experienced a psychotic breakdown. It is all he can do to say he is sorry and hopes Megan is ok. He actually keeps calling her Naomi and doesn't really know what's going on at the moment. Aiden also would not be returning to this rehab."

"Well, the shocks keep piling up don't they," said someone. "Is it always like this?"

Wolfie replies "Sometimes the insanity of an addict's thought patterns can be easily seen in the behaviours they engage in. These crazy behaviours make little sense to anyone who is not using or does not understand the illness. This crazy behaviour is common and all too familiar to staff working with addiction."

"Both Megan and Aiden are safe, and we are all thankful about that." Offers Sindy.

"Well I'm bloody well pissed off with the pair of them," said Brendon. "We listened to both their stories and told them ours. We expect nothing from each other, but this really does feel like a betrayal."

"I don't feel betrayed I said, I do feel sad. Sad that Megan just continued to act like a child, running away because she didn't like meetings. (realising how it might look if anyone had known of my desire to run away, or the car, or the breaking of rules.). I just feel confused about Aiden being so bloody stupid by taking off with a young woman, and also for taking that cocktail of drugs, knowing what might happen."

"Ah," said Wolfie," perhaps he didn't know what would happen, he had of course been taking copious amounts of all sorts of things for a long time. He then suffered a trauma as you know with the drug dealers, and then also has had a couple of weeks of clean time. I don't think Aiden had any idea that he was lighting an explosive episode by doing what he did. He's actually lucky to be alive, as the mixture of things he took, especially after a period of being clean, could have very well killed him. As it is he has barely survived with his mind intact. It will take some time for him to regain some semblance of mental health."

"We do have to reiterate," said Sindy, "that Abstinence is the key to anything that might improve your lives. Whatever is going on in your lives, a fear of meetings, of speaking in public, a relationship breakup and so on… cannot be fixed by using. If you do not learn this piece of the puzzle and adhere to it, you will forever be caught up in mad stories such as we have just heard."

"So, did all of this happen because Megan was scared about going to meetings?" I asked.

"I would think so," said Sindy "but also about many more things she heard in treatment; the meeting's question was only the tip of an iceberg. If you remember she said she couldn't practice abstinence around relationships, and for a nineteen-year-old, the difficulty in altering everything you do in a social setting looks impossible. She didn't say it, but most likely felt like most of us do at first, that life would be boring, and she would have no friends or fun anymore."

"Well I must admit I have felt like this at times," I said. "But then the memory of my so-called social life and all the horrible things that have happened in it remind me it wasn't so great. So the thought of changing it and myself, actually looks quite appealing."

For the first time in many days I allowed myself to think about JT, the love of my life, the man I had been waiting for the night of my last blackout and wild ride to rehab. I had no idea what he thought, if he knew where I was, or what to do about him or anything else.

"You look very sad," say the therapists, "don't worry too much about Megan and Aiden they will be taken care of."

"I am thinking about Megan and Aiden but also about myself and my man JT."

"Strewth Blue, you kept him quiet!" says Brendon, again sounding very Australian as surprise ran round the group about my revelation about JT.

"I didn't know what to say about him, and you must admit it's been a bit busy with different stuff going on."

"Yes it has been a bit hectic," says Wolfie, "but Mimi, you really do have to tell your story. We can then help you figure out what should happen next about JT as well as the rest of your life. We have heard you had a bit of a meltdown last night, so it is time to talk. Nothing changes if nothing changes."

Oh no! Me and my big mouth, I should've kept quiet. I wanted to roar a **no I won't tell you anything,** but a meek little okay actually came out of my mouth.

Maybe I can disappear I thought to myself, then no-one needs hear this bloody boring tale of mine.

I go back to my room and continue to think about all the things that had happened here at Moriatta Falls in such a short space of time. I never realised that rehab would be like this. I honestly thought it was all about not using, which of course it was, but there was so much more involved. I learnt that my biggest problem was the way I thought, and my thinking was the thing that controlled my behaviours. My behaviours had been so shameful that my self-esteem and self-respect reached rock bottom. Some of the things that had happened and some of the things talked about by the others, seemed almost unreal, but also I identified with most of it. It didn't shock me particularly. But witnessing everyone else's madness enabled me for the first time to really understand how the people in my life like my mother or JT might have felt. This revelation saddened me. As JT's face swam into my mind I really began to miss him, his comforting arms and generous spirit. His ability to make me laugh when I was down. I don't think he ever told me not to use, and he sometimes joined me in a crazy night out, but as I thought harder I realised that whilst my using was out of control, his wasn't.

I was the addict, he wasn't. Strange I had never thought of this before, just took for granted everything that went down in our relationship was a shared experience. I remembered my last shameful night of 'freedom' before I got to rehab, the fact that JT might have to know about this filled my whole body with shame. I cringed and told myself I would never tell him, or anyone come to that. After all I'm the 'good girl' I know how to be invisible, I know how to hide in plain sight. Hatching this plan made me feel better, braver. I can do this I thought.

15: Vanda the Girl in Flight

As we gathered for group again there was a kind of lottery about who would be telling their story next, I managed to get myself some extra time telling the team that after last night I felt so ill. My eyes were still red and my face puffy, so they knew I wasn't blagging it.

Bet I look real cute I thought, always self-obsessed even in this mad circumstance.

Vanda said I'm ready to do it.

Vanda

Nothing about the start I had in life would make anyone think that what happened to me later in life would happen. My childhood was unremarkable, school was ok, I had a penchant for mathematical equations which made me quite popular with the other kids as it happens. That was lucky because my name, being different, caused a bit of commotion at times. So I was always a little self-conscious. Family life was great really, with my parents encouraging me all the way to follow my dreams. One of my dreams was to travel and see the world, and I figured out the best way to do this was to become a flight attendant on a swanky airliner and get paid to see the world. Becoming a pilot, she said, was a bit beyond me, my co-ordination was slightly askew, she laughed as she said this.

Things in my life started to unravel a bit when I discovered gambling some years ago. I had become head supervisor at work and was responsible for my team, sales and passengers. My problems started on a stopover one weekend whilst we were in Dubai, the crew had time on their hands. I was never one for drinking much so I was at a loose end and bored. When someone suggested going to a casino I jumped at the chance. Well, it was like walking into another world, a beautiful room with well-dressed people. Nothing brash or brazen in this world. Soft sounds in the background, attentive waiters serving coffee or whatever we wanted. My first roll of the dice won big, and my luck that night continued. My companions were astonished at what was going on, and just like in the movies I had people gathered around watching me roll the dice and win. My adrenalin was pumping and the feeling in me and in the room was electric. I had no idea I could do this and if truth be known I had no idea how I was doing it, but that first night when I discovered gambling it was magic and when we left the casino I had a few thousand dollars in my bag. Reality was a little deflating as we had to go straight back on duty and look after an aircraft full of demanding people.

I wish I could tell you that this was my success story about gambling, and if I had stopped here it would have been a brilliant story. However the story goes downhill from now on. Every time we flew into Dubai I would end up in the casino, I became quite well known and they would greet me by name. Sometimes I would win again, but never like that first time. Along with my new hobby came other things of course. I needed to look the part. I was mixing with some pretty wealthy people, so I started to buy expensive clothes and accessories, of course we were on a stopover in one of the best retail havens in the world, so this part was easy. The next thing that happened was I met women who were into the body beautiful, and they told me of procedures that cost next to nothing but would enhance my look. Before I knew it, I was spending money I didn't have on cosmetic surgery. Expensive clothes, gambling and surgery, really it never ended. I could still be lucky in the casino and would win, but gradually my expenditures far exceeded my incomings.

My habit continued even at home in England, I would bet on the most ridiculous online sites, I would play fruit machines, anything. The old story really, I got into debt, trying to fund my fairy tale life. As my debts and loans mounted I devised a way of 'borrowing' money at work. I was responsible for some pretty big sums of money on the trips to foreign shores, I always meant to pay it back but somehow this also got out of control. I was caught red-handed and with no reasonable explanation, I am at the moment awaiting a court date to answer to my charges of theft and fraud. I've been suspended of course, and I don't think I can stand to live with the shame I feel. My family have all rallied round to give me this chance to get better. They knew I was depressed and close to ending it all.

The hush in the room was thick and could be cut with a knife, Vanda was white as a sheet. She had begun to cry quietly.

"Well done Vanda," said Wolfie, "that was some story. Thank you for being so open, we can all see what telling the story has done to you. Even though behavioural addictions seem different, the devastation and progression downward are the same as for substance abuse. With gambling it always seems to follow a familiar route, fun, excitement, winning then losing. Your logical, rational thinking becomes distorted as you try to chase the money you have lost. In your case you also started to develop a spending habit, and your body dysmorphia and Bulimia all conspired with the gambling to take you to a very dangerous state of mind. Not so very different to what addiction to substances does. The same chemical spikes in your brain occur." Wolfie paused to enable Vanda to blow her nose and take a drink of water.

"What the group don't know is that you have been working with us for some time before your admission here. You have become aware there are things like **Gamstop** and **Gamcare** which are organisations that offer advice and help you to block and prevent access to all kinds of gambling sites. You have unsubscribed to all the different places people like to gamble at and in as well as coming into treatment. Vanda, you have become part of the solution now. You have lost your job so no more Dubai which is sad but necessary. I don't know what will happen about court, you may be facing a prison sentence but coming here and addressing the problem head-on is a great first step in the many you will have to take to Recovery. We at Moriatta Falls will be doing all we can with reports and recommendations to your solicitor to try to help you."

"So group, what kind of support can you give Vanda?"

"I've never heard a gamblers story before," says Pavla. "Thank you Vanda, it's not so different to my story really is it? You ended up in exactly the same place as I did. I'm just lucky I don't have any serious charges to answer to, my ending up in jail was a once-only holding cell until I sobered up. I've still got a whole mess of stuff to deal with Marco though, he's definitely not in a forgiving mood. I suppose anyone would be angry at a crazy woman screaming she wanted to kill you. But I don't know how I would cope if I had a court date hanging over my head."

We all gathered around poor, sad Vanda, thanking her and trying to support her.

"Blimey," says Brendon, "what was all that cosmetic stuff and Bulimia about? You're gorgeous and don't need any of that shit."

"Thank you," says Vanda, "but I don't really understand why exactly I did all the things I did. But I don't feel very gorgeous, never have really. The Bulimia started whilst I was at school as a way of keeping my weight down, I've always hated the way I look. The surgery was bloody mad. I can see that now. I just wanted to be seen as one of the 'beautiful people'."

"Remember," says Wolfie, "things don't follow a logical route in our illnesses. Vanda was feeling out of control, and managing her weight and looks is the simplest way to understand what happened to her, it doesn't matter that we all think Vanda is lovely, it's what she feels inside that drove her to do what she did. Feelings of powerlessness and unmanageability are never easy to deal with."

"God, you are so lovely Vanda, I hate to think of you going to jail." Says Rita.

"I don't really know what's going to happen, my company are being quite supportive actually, but it just depends on how I do here and what my solicitor can make happen for me. Coming to treatment was a stipulation from the airline as well as my parents. Everyone wants me to do well. I feel pretty terrible at the moment, I am so ashamed of stealing from the company, but I don't feel suicidal anymore. I really am thankful to everyone for trying to help me and I do feel that solutions can be found. If I end up in jail so be it, que sera sera, as they say. I will survive it."

16: Characteristics of a Functional Family

Sindy who was taking this group said that first of all to really understand the impact we have on family and friends; we have to know what constitutes a functional family. Our lives were all vastly different and some of us had really messed up with different partners, or trouble with the kids etc. but we all had some idea what a happy family 'looked' like

She asked us to name some characteristics we thought should be in place for 'happy' to happen.

We shouted out different things and Sindy wrote them down in columns on the whiteboard.

Honesty and Truth

Love and Affection

Trust and Responsibility

Openness and Availability

Sharing and Participation

Loyalty and Faithfulness

Support and Encouragement

Safety and Security

We all knew what we wanted and desired in a functional family it seems. Sindy's next instructions however blew us away, she asked us to list what our lives in and around our addictions was like for us or for everyone else we said we loved. None of us had much trouble talking about some of the trail of destruction and pain we had left in our wake.

> **Dishonesty and deviousness**
>
> **Lack of communication and Secrecy**
>
> **Mistrust and Fear**
>
> **Lack of support and Selfishness**
>
> **Dishonour and Disharmony**
>
> **Contempt and Disdain**
>
> **Smoke and Mirrors**
>
> **Infidelity and Unfaithfulness**
>
> **Misery and Unhappiness**

The list was as long if not longer than the first one, however as soon as we realised what we were saying we were not so enthusiastic.

"God," said someone, "we're talking about our lives here, how is it we couldn't see it properly?"

"None of this was rocket science," said Sindy, "but knowing it all gives everyone in the family an idea of what has to be repaired once someone gets into recovery. The reason you haven't really noticed has something to do with that little word that pops up in addiction very often **DENIAL –** a brilliant explanation of this word is: **'sincerely believing our own lies'**"

A dictionary explanation includes: 'refutation, rebuttal, disclaimer, negation' and so it goes on.

Sindy continues this talk with,

It is hard and almost impossible for an addict to change and grow in recovery unless the family want to go along for the ride. Very often she added they certainly do not want to make any changes themselves. 'Why the hell should I?' is often the response, I've had to put up with all the crazy behaviour first of all with your addiction and now I have to change my...
social habits,
stop having alcohol in the house,
not go on holiday
forgive you!...

and all the rest of the changes that need to happen to enable recovery to grow. Who the hell do you think you are? Everything is always all about you'

Family or significant others are usually pretty hurt and angry by the time you reach Rehab. It is essential that they too have access to counselling and treatment. In some cases their attendance at our Family Support Group will help educate and help them understand what has been going on, however in some cases it is too little too late.

We always tell you we have no idea if your marriages or relationships can be saved, all we can do is teach **you** about addiction, break down **your** denial and give as much support as we can to your family. There is actually much work to be done in this area of your lives. There are many support services for family members or friends, we have brochures and handouts that we can send out informing them of all of this if you want us to. Like I said, it is very hard to change unless our loved ones come on board and become part of the change.

Sindy continues:

We all know what addiction looks like. We read stories about it, we watch movies and news articles about the drug epidemic, we know about drunk or drugged drivers and the carnage created. We may even know a few addicts whose behaviour we avoid. What we don't know is how to deal with the addict in our own families. The emphasis always seems to be on the problems and not really the solution. Yes of course the addict needs to stop using and everyone knows they don't want to.

It is the 'don't want to' statement that causes the problems. Some addicts of course don't want to, but some don't know how to stop and stay stopped. They will continue to not want to, until they find out how to, or that they need to.

The other problem is of course this whole thing about enabling. It seems like a family member or concerned other is being blamed when the enabling statement occurs. So what is enabling?

When the addict's behaviours are being covered up.

But cover-ups happen to protect the jobs, to protect the finances, to protect the reputations, and protect the family.

When excuses are made about the money that has been spent on any of the addictions.

Believing the problem is depression, or anxiety or lost jobs, or a bad childhood.

It is really a question of different language that is being spoken. The family member and society know the problem is the using, the addict believes the using is the solution. Plus the solution about addiction cannot come from the addicted mind, it has to come from outside of the addict. If we all speak different languages then a solution will be an impossibility. We all have to begin to find a way to understand each other and begin to speak the same language. This is often seen as a 'cop-out' or some such insulting idea, yet in treatment when the addict is 'forced' to face their behaviour, and the truth with solutions is talked about, many addicts are able to at last see and work on the solutions.

In any other illness, the sick person and family members have big resources to aid and support them, but where addiction is concerned the right support is often not available. Or the shame about the illness stops the right kind of help from being found. Secrecy and lies, and smoke and mirrors. This aspect of the disease permeates every single aspect of the subject.

The addicted person cannot 'just stop', or choose to say no, or cut back and be ok, or drink like a lady or gamble like a gentleman. In a world that believes these things, is it any wonder the addict 'gets away' so often with terrible behaviour.

On the one hand we have a society that makes alcohol the cheapest and most easily obtained drug in the world, and an attitude that glamorises the party lifestyle. Gambling is the easiest thing to engage in these days especially with the internet. We think it's cool to drink everyone under the table. We make it easy yet slam the people who can't control themselves. We have a society of double standards in everything to do with addiction. It's an illness, yet we criminalise the users. I realise this is a hot subject, but we manage to tightly control and monitor many medications and do not look down on the people who need them. Something needs to change in our thinking about it all.

Perceptions about the disease have to change. In treatment, or at Anonymous meetings, or in counselling the change of perception begins. If EVERYONES perceptions, and that is everyones perceptions, could change, then perhaps we would be getting somewhere with this problem of addiction in our society.

17: Rick's Unhealthy Game

Rick is the next one to present to the group, he offered, I continue to try to hide.

"Mimi you must stop hiding," say the therapists "we will give you one more day to prepare your story and then you really have to talk. Nothing can change for you until you start communicating and looking for ways to change direction in your life. You cannot do that without help, and we cannot help you unless you talk. The thing to remember is that no-one but you blames you for ending up in rehab, this silence from you is rather worrying."

"Okay, okay, okay," I say, "I know this bit is about surrender and asking for help, it's just so hard to do."

"Yes it is," says Wolfie, "perhaps one the hardest things ever, but once you do it, all sorts of things start to happen. It's the start of a verbal testimony to the fact that you realise you had no control, and that your life is or was unmanageable because of it, and you know you need help. Everything you might have tried, if you did, was pointless, you couldn't remain clean from your addictions no matter how hard you tried."

"Oh I know I need help; I just feel so ashamed of myself."

"We know kid," says Brendon kindly, "but look we've all done it, we've all survived, and I'm betting you don't think less of us, despite some of the things we've done?"

"True Brendon, it just feels different when it's me."

"Well," says Wolfie, "one more day Mimi, then you really must talk," he says this kindly so although it was a direct order of sorts, I didn't actually mind or feel rebellious. Even I felt I needed to bloody well get this story told. I promised myself I would cut the crap and do it next time I was asked. Surprising myself by not plotting my escape. It was time anyhow to live up to my promise to the universe.

Rick

My greatest wish in the whole world when I was a kid was to play football, I was pretty good at it, and my parents encouraged me all the way. When I got talent-spotted early on, everyone, but especially me was over the moon. I left home and was taken under the wing of _____ and Rick said the name of a club we had all heard of.

We all became quite impressed then, although I for one had not recognised Rick, but then me and footie were not friends!

I felt everything in my life was perfect says Rick. I trained hard and those early years were a blur of achievements and going up the ladder in the club. I was being picked to play more and more important games. Along with all of this came financial rewards as well. My career in the club was stellar. I was one of their star player's, so I was looked after pretty well. I was only twenty and was able to buy my parents a lovely house. I met a great girl, we got married, bought our own house and our lovely baby girl was born.

I was never a big drinker, and I stayed clear of all the drugs that were easy access to us players. I also tried to stay clear of all the women that threw themselves at us but have to confess to my shame, I broke my marriage vows once or twice. It was all too easy to live in a fantasy world, where reality did not exist. There were no characteristics of any kind of functioning family. Lots of lies, smoke and mirrors, like Sindy said in her lecture.

My biggest buzz though seemed to come from the matches themselves, to hear my name being screamed out by a stadium full of fans was awesome, I loved it, we got some abuse too but it all just added to the adrenalin rush of match days. Another adrenalin rush I loved came from gambling, I remember betting insane amounts of money, and playing, like Vanda, in places all around the world. I loved that feeling too, or at least I did when I was winning, but days came when I blew everything and had to get advances at work. My wife started to get suspicious about my late nights. One of the women was threatening exposure through the media. I had to pay her to keep it quiet. I couldn't bear the thought of my wife finding out.

The shine of course went away from my marriage and our lives together. I adored our little girl but couldn't wait to get out to whatever poker night or casino outing was being planned. The other women were just a part of this world, that actually never felt real. Because of my late nights, my training suffered, which meant the game I loved also suffered. Without really realising it I was losing everything I held dear.

Betting for me was an outlet, I felt I worked hard and provided well for my family, so I deserved a little fun. Well as you can imagine my family, and my manager, and the team wouldn't and couldn't put up with my arrogant attitude for much longer. I was given so many chances by both the club and my wife, but I didn't listen. I sometimes wanted to stop, but like I've heard you all say I couldn't. There was always one more sure bet, or can't lose situation, the anticipation was obsessive. I'm now facing a disciplinary and fine at work.

I guess that is why I'm here, my wife's last ultimatum has finally penetrated, she said she would leave permanently with our child if I don't get help. I came home last week to an empty house with a note telling me to get help or she wasn't coming back. She won't take my telephone calls. My manager and the boys are all pissed off with me too, I've missed too many training sessions.

My career is at a stage where I should be thinking of retiring from the game and doing something else. I should have money put aside for this day, but I haven't, luckily my house is paid for and in our joint names, and I have a few investments that I've been unable to cash in, so I'm not completely broke. My wife leaving me has brought me to my senses. I've realised she and our kid are what is important. I want a chance to get them back and I'll do anything to make that happen.

Rick stops suddenly, he is shaking and looks ready to cry.

"Well done Rick," says Wolfie, "you have been very open with us, what I heard is that your world is an extremely disciplined one and your training regime very hard. It wouldn't surprise me if as well as gambling, you were also addicted to exercise and maybe also have a sex addiction. These are called cross addictions, and many people have more than one thing that they become addicted to."

"I didn't know such things existed," said Vanda. "I thought sex-addiction was just some excuse people used for selfish behaviour. Seems a bit of a cop-out to call sex an addiction."

"Could be, I guess," says Jake pitching in," but I promise you the behaviour is anything but nice, its desperate and usually quite sordid. Remember the blackmailing women too, no-one would bring that on themselves for fun. I love my wife very much and now in the cold light of day cannot believe I acted the way I did."

Hamish also added, "Perhaps the exercise stuff was the same type of discipline I had most of my working life, very timetabled, precise and long hours."

Wolfie said, "You are completely right, and addicts have very obsessive-compulsive tendencies a lot of the time. Rick had also spoken about the adrenalin rush he got from a stadium full of people calling his name, anyone in the spotlight, such as musicians and actors for instance can also identify with that adrenalin rush. The highs and lows of it all contribute to the progression of addiction if that illness is present."

"Interesting isn't it?" says Rita," none of us had heard too much about gambling or sex addiction, then two of each come along close together."

"Life is a bit like that at times. A bit like buses as they say, but really It's once you know about something, you tend to see and hear more about it," says Wolfie.

As we all troop out to the smoking pit and coffee room everyone is chitchatting away about all the different experiences that have been exposed about our lives.

Rita is talking about her imminent discharge from treatment. She has completed all the different things we each have to complete. Her husband has been to the family group and they have talked and agreed to make some changes at home. Her two girls are going to go for some counselling, and they have had days out. Rita has even had an overnight stay at home, which went well.

She addresses me specifically saying, "Mimi if you don't share soon, I won't be here to hear or support you, and I want to do that. I was here when you first arrived, and I can see all the improvements and changes that have happened in your stay. I really want to be around to hear your story."

"Wolfie said Mimi's share was this afternoon," says Brendon.

"Great," says Rita, smiling at me.

Shit! thinks I maybe there is still time to get the hell out of dodge. Making a joke which surprises me as I feel that what is about to happen is anything but a joke.

But I do want Rita to be around to support me, we have become quite friendly during the days in group navigating the crazy lives of ourselves and everyone else. Rita the oracle has proved to be a bit of a godsend to me. Always having a kind word and listening ear to my fears and worries. She also let me advise and support her in some things, which is unbelievably amazing. Being able to help someone else and say the thing that brings clarity is the commodity I have come to love about group work. Hating group first of all but now seeing how it works and appreciating it. Wolfie also says that we can all be wise for each other, we just come unstuck when we try to be wise for ourselves. Weird but true! I still don't relish the thought of THE STORY, but guess I have to suck it up and get on with it. Even I'm fed up with my dodging the subject.

18: The Invisible Child Made Visible

I don't know why I'm making such a fuss; I say as my mouth dries and my heart races. The gang place tissues and water near my feet and Wolfie gently tells me to take my time, stop if need be, practice breathing slowly, like in your yoga classes.

Yeah well, you've all heard some of the stupid stuff that went on in my early life. This illness was part of my childhood and showed itself in my father's behaviour and in the lifestyle we all had as kids. My mother was a warrior, she kept us safe really and took the brunt of his rage. She really is my heroine, the woman I most admire in the world. She was strong and fierce and when he left she made sure we all stayed together. It could have been very different because he left us without much support. I don't know where he is these days, married his fourth wife I think, but shit who cares about him.

My teenage years were where I discovered substances and despite my disdain at my old man's behaviour took to it all without a second thought. I never believed I was like him at all. I was a kind of dreamy girl, loved Tolkien and all things magic. Fairies and festivals and that kind of thing. Early on I had a wandering spirit and took off travelling, did all kinds of jobs and basically felt life was ok most of the time. For someone so shy and introverted though I have no idea how I managed to do all that travelling, but somehow I liked being a loner. I had friends and boyfriends but nothing very permanent. Until JT came along, I fell madly in love with him, we kind of just drifted along I always kept in touch with my mother and siblings, but really JT was my raison d'etre. He comforted me and looked out for me when my behaviour got too bad. The thing that catapulted my using was when my brother was killed on his motorbike. We had been talking about doing some travelling together, the day it happened I was in some other country making plans to see him soon. My world crashed with the news he had died. I remember thinking I'm going to get 'out of it' and that's exactly what I did. It was always my favourite term about using, now I wonder exactly what I was trying to get out of? I stayed 'out of it' however. Maybe it was my mind I wanted out of, or the world, but most definitely reality. Despite my horrible blackouts I continued to use anything to accomplish my mission of 'getting out of it' I just got sicker and sicker and the shit just piled up. I couldn't even go to my brothers funeral because I didn't have the money to get home in time. My relationship with JT and my love for my mother were the only things keeping me anchored to the earth.

There's nothing more really to say, I told you it was a boring old story. I used too many drugs and alcohol and got sick – the end – I hate myself and my life so much – I want to disappear – at the moment I want to leave and find some other place to be, but I know from listening to all of you I can't keep running, I have to somehow start resolving this shit, that is something I have learned already. - There, the end.

As the tears slid down my face, the group's presence felt comforting to me. When I calmed a little Wolfie started with the usual congrats at my bravery.

I don't feel very brave, I said "plus there's another bit to my story which I haven't told yet, for the longest time whilst I have been here I thought I had killed someone with my car. I noticed what I thought was blood in the dents when I went to get my credit cards. I didn't say anything and had to go out to look properly to make sure a few days ago. After checking though I have realised it was dried berry juice in the dents. Yes I did break the rules about not going out the building, but I had to check."

"You know Mimi, bravery is all about facing your own particular challenges, it's not about how bad something is compared to someone else's bad, but as you said in your story, being able to stop running away and facing head-on the things you have run from all your life. Some rules are worth breaking sometimes I guess, and I will honestly say I would have done the same as you to check my car. I'm sure the parallels between your accident and your brothers crash are not lost on you. However back to your history."

"Your father's addiction was very damaging to you and all your family; you have a lot of work to do about these family relationships, but you can see from the way you react to his memory how damaging addiction is in family life. Nature or nurture doesn't really matter does it? It's damaging and ugly and requires a lot of specific work.

Your admiration and respect and love for your mother is, I believe, beautiful and shows what is important to you. The death of your brother is a huge loss in your life, a life of many losses actually, but this one seemingly has sent you over the edge. It seems almost an arbitrary thing that we are here talking about addiction. I believe your addiction may have saved you strangely, without it your inability to cope with yourself and your life may have led to your taking your own life. You coincidently heard the talk about suicide awareness early on in your stay. You know what we always say here? Nothing really happens by chance. Every experience that occurs at Moriatta Falls is a piece of a puzzle you all have to construct to make a cohesive picture. Happily you have now found us and have a chance at Recovery. Substances no longer work for you if they ever did, so it is time to change direction. You called yourself an invisible child early on in your stay, well my dear, you have just stopped running long enough to become solid and real. Well done."

The group all join Wolfie in saying comforting things.

To be honest I can't really hear too much. My head is foggy and can't seem to hold on to much. But I stay seated in my chair, stay rooted in the group room and piece by piece my body emerges into the here and now. I know there is much work still to do on all of the things Wolfie mentioned and even more as I think of JT but for today at least I have begun to believe I can exist in the world, without any form of running away.

"God I didn't think I could do that;" I say to my peers.

"Well you did," says Rita as she hugs me, "and what's more we knew you could. Welcome to our world Mimi."

"You're a bit of a dark horse though aren't you?" says Hamish, "who would have thought a 'good girl' like you, would break some rules. I like that best about your story."

I laugh and shoot Brendon a conspiritual glance. He comes over and gives me the biggest hug, whispering, "Thanks for not giving me away."

No judgement, no recrimination, no blame, simply understanding and acceptance from a bunch of strangers who knew what I felt and had gone through.

19: Endings, New Beginnings - Repeat

My metamorphosis into a real live present human continued throughout my stay at the clinic. The rest of the journey although not easy was never as hard as this first bit of the fight for redemption and renewal. Every journey starts with the first step said someone famous one time, and that is certainly true in Moriatta Falls and in every rehab in the world and in every story of Recovery. We have to admit we can't do a thing about the problem ourselves alone and recognise that because of it our lives are insanely out of control. It wasn't so hard to admit in the end, I had recognised the devastation in my life for a long time. What was hard, was forming the words and telling the peers and therapists. My shame about my behaviour was so great it threatened to annihilate me.

The next thing I and my peers needed was to formulate how on earth to remain focused on staying clean and sober and work out who or what was going to help. This is the time some people run away from the 12-step way of doing things because it sounds like and feels like religion is being offered. For some people who have a God faith I guess it is like that, but for me and countless others like me with no particular God faith, the task of finding something to believe in is given to us. Ideas of who was going to help included the treatment centre we had all washed up in, with all the counsellors and peers who wanted to make the journey with us. Some did and we stayed connected, some didn't want this new way of living and relapsed.

We all had to find ways to forgive and let go of our past. We had to become responsible for our own actions. I realised I had blamed my upbringing for all sorts of things but especially for my using of all kinds of substances. This had to stop as the substances themselves were now causing worse mayhem than my upbringing. As long as I blamed something or someone else I remained stuck in the problem. With my newfound responsibility I discovered that forgiveness set me free. If I could forgive not just the past and its people then I also could forgive me. I had not really known what I was unleashing in myself when I took my first substance. I did not realise that addiction was an illness and that continued use would become out of control. I also understood what Wolfie said about having needed the addiction to cope with myself and life. Strange but true. I was now learning new ways to cope with life, getting an education about things I did not even know I was deficient in.

Saying goodbye to peers who had taken this journey with me was tough sometimes, especially as some of them, as we shall see did not make it. That statement makes it sound like recovery is a bit of a lottery, well, it does look like it sometimes. But the truth of the matter is that every relapse has a reason for it to happen in the first place. We are taught a set of principles and guidelines to live by, it is up to us if we live by them. If we do, we formulate our own new standards to live by, if we don't, we fall into the abyss again, where anything goes, and survival of this place is uncertain. What is certain though, is that we unleash the madness and insanity again and formulating the healthy selves we all say we want is unbelievably hard, especially hard if we have a head full of therapy and 'recovery' Relapses always looked and sounded painful, if a person made it back to recovery they never told us it had been wonderful and fun. It was always painful, shameful, hard and depressing. Some of course never made it back.

Everybody's stories created and formulated pieces of the puzzle, the bits they turned over in their stories formed other bits, and in the end what was revealed was what should have been from the start. Some, like me find this revelation to be precious.

Rita the oracle, is unable to be forgiven by her husband, he blames her drinking for everything broken in their marriage. He is unable to leave his pretty young mistress who comforted him whilst Rita is in treatment. Rita re-connects with her two daughters. The three of them live in relative calmness whilst Rita divorces her cheating spouse. With the help of Moriatta Falls and a lot of on-going counselling she is able to work through the pain and anger this evokes in her. She remains clean and sober and a great supporter of Moriatta Falls. Her oracle like tendencies are put to great use by all of us. Rita and I become great friends and she lets me meet her lovely daughters. We both tell the tale of my haphazard way of ending up in Moriatta

Falls. The 60-mile drive in blackout has become one of the legends of the place.

Brendon decides he wants to re-locate near to the clinic. Cold old England grows on him and he wants to stay. He reluctantly lets go of his quest to find Pattie and decides to annul his marriage. In doing so he sets himself free and remains clean and sober. He plans to train as a therapist when he has some clean time under his belt. In the meantime his brilliance with cars gets him a job in some millionaires garage, where he looks after six or seven luxury cars. He loves it and is happy tinkering around. He decides to get in touch with his parents, who are overjoyed to hear from their long-lost son. Sindy works with all of them as a family to try to heal some of the rift. It is a rocky road but Brendon's up for the challenge.

Aiden is last heard of catching an overnight ferry to Rotterdam. He escapes from hospital before the police, Megan's folks or anyone can question him. He leaves no note and does not phone anyone. Everyone and especially Brendon is disappointed he has blown us all off. Sobriety status and whereabouts unknown. His violent drug tale is another of those legends.

Megan does well in her second rehab, comes back to the UK and visits Moriatta Falls to apologise to the staff and all of us from her group. She said she can't explain her actions. She believes she had fallen in love with Aiden or was temporarily mad! She said she didn't even really know him but their plans to run away were exciting at the time. She had no idea taking drugs would send him crazy and had been very frightened. Wolfie says this is just another example of the insanity of the disease of addiction. Twisted thinking and twisted behaviour. Megan stays clean and sober and goes back to her studies at University. She comes to aftercare on a regular basis, she says it is one of her favourite meetings. She still loves spiders. She promises all of us that she doesn't collect them anymore. The legend of her pets is one of the favourites when it is told. We all remember the shudders we had, and the new people can imagine them.

Pavla and her husband Marco have relationship counselling and reunite. They discover her desire to kill Marco was all to do with her confused thoughts and feelings about her father. These revelations in relationship counselling are hard but effective, more examples of the twisted thinking in addiction. Marco forgives her. Their business goes from strength to strength and they decide to go back to live in Bulgaria to be with Pavla's Grandmother, who although pretty old now is a great help with their on-line clothing business. Pavla stays sober and loves the meetings in Bulgaria. She visits Aftercare whenever she can.

Hamish completes treatment and goes on to be a regular at Aftercare. He uses his lecturing skills to talk about Relapse and Recovery, joining AA's scheme to take the word about Recovery into prisons and schools. He is enjoying his retirement and his newfound interests in life. He and his family are having extensive on-going therapy and they are working through their angst. He has been invited back to his old University to talk about addictions and Recovery. He always says if his story can help just one other person, he will die happy. Hamish is helping many more people who hear his story.

Vanda completes treatment and with her efforts coupled with the clinic's help avoids a jail sentence. She stops gambling but is unable to curb her cosmetic surgery addiction. After a botched lip filler incident she stops coming to Aftercare. We hear she met an old flame from Dubai and runs away with him. She has relapsed with cosmetic surgery. Her parents still come to the Family support group, they say she seems happy, has not started gambling again, but also that she refuses to return to England. They say she can't bear the thought of people seeing her ruined face. The staff are working on trying to get Vanda to visit or at least talk to the team. She's pretty elusive however, so it is a slow process.

Jake and Graham part ways after a few months of counselling. Jake remains sober despite his sorrow at losing his marriage. He sells his share of the business to Graham and they remain amicable. He goes onto develop a new career in sober entertainment and is very successful. He hosts huge festival-type events, which are all the rage, in people looking for a clean sober safe life. In recovery he has discovered pride in himself again. He continues to attend Aftercare and other meetings; he is a huge help to the therapy team when anyone with similar addictions to his come into the clinic. Chem sex is still a bit of a taboo subject and hard for people to own up to. His experience ends up helping many. He says he has looked for something like that all his life. He is happy and content to remain single, much to his amazement.

Rick works hard in treatment and he and his wife re-unite. His little girl remains the apple of his eye. He starts to coach young rising stars of the football world, as well as being a supporter of Moriatta Falls Aftercare. He does some voluntary work for the centre and his story is always an inspiration for the newbies in treatment. The blackmailing women have all disappeared from his radar. Now that he is clean he is no longer afraid. He says they can tell they would not gain much by threatening him. His wife knows all of his story, and with the therapists help they have both come to terms with it.

Pete's memory is honoured through the planting of a rose bush in the gardens of Moriatta Falls. All of his in-patient group contribute to the bush and a plaque, everyone who is able meets up for a small ceremony. Pete's parents and sister are invited and are overwhelmed by the support they receive. They are saddened but also gladdened by this gesture for their son and brother. Pete is never forgotten by any of us, a sad but powerful reminder of how badly life can go wrong. Often singly or as a group we will gather round his rose bush which flowers with the most lovely yellow blooms which smell amazing. We remember him with sadness and our start on the recovery journey. His story symbolises so much to us. So close to a solution but so far from being able to have it. We have all witnessed many examples of this in different stories. We who have found the solution are often reminded by Pete's memory to be grateful for what we have found.

The person made visible - I finished treatment, with lots of tears but no more tantrums. JT was invited to a meeting with Sindy. JT refused to come to the meeting, he said he understood and loved me, but then he also said he no longer wanted to be with me. He couldn't come to terms with the label of addict, and also did not want to stop using himself. This nearly made me disappear again, but I held on tight to the sanity I had discovered, and even tighter to the people I had decided would help me. My 'Power Greater' The therapy team requested that JT wrote a letter to me in order to help me 'let go' I didn't want to hear the things he said, but again, once it was all said and out in the open, it helped.

Dearest Mimi,

I first want to tell you how very proud I am of you for making this first move to sobriety. I never thought you would do it as you had avoided all talk about stopping using for so long. It is really the length of the problems we have had that are pushing me to make this move away from you. It is very sad that at the point of your being able to change, I feel I have had enough of the life we had together. I am so sorry Mimi, but I cannot forgive your last crazy behaviour before you landed in Moriatta Falls. It is just the end result of many similar episodes that have been hard to handle. My fear and worry about you were never enough to stop your behaviour.

I know you don't have a bad bone in your body but sweetheart when you are 'out of it' you are horrible. You spend money we don't have; you lie about who and what you have been up to and you say the most vile things to me, which you never remember. Whenever we have tried to repair some of this damage in the past you always make the excuse and say that blackouts are the problem. No my love, your drinking is/was the problem. Hopefully you can now change all of this. You must hold onto your recovery; I don't think you will survive too many more episodes with

strange guys picking you up. Yes I know about the ship and that last night before rehab. I'm not holding that against you, but as I said it is just the last thing in a long line of things that are wrong in our relationship. Please don't try to find me, I am leaving the country and flying to Nepal for a trek into the mountains. I need to clear my head of us and you. I wish you only love and peace Mimi.

- JT

This letter was sent and read a few days after I told my story to the group. The therapy team said I did not have to read it out in group as most of the letters from home were. This was a goodbye letter and as such need not be shared unless I wanted to. I spent hours talking and crying about the contents. Berating myself for not acting sooner. Thinking that if I had, my relationship may have survived.

The group rallied round, the therapy team did what they did best and supported and listened. Until gradually I became calm and rationale. I was able to begin to view my relationship with JT in a more realistic way. I remained sad but determined that this break up should not derail my fledgeling recovery.

Brendon and I became the best of friends and propped each other up in our similar heartbreak. We stayed faithful to the programme though and never crossed those boundaries into something more exotic. We had both discovered we loved Recovery and would do anything to preserve it. We knew that creating more than friendship at this time would give even bigger problems for both of us, and neither of us wished to chance it. Our escapade of breaking the rules and setting my guilt-free became another one of those legends which we told to a select few. We never told the staff the whole story but were never exactly sure if they didn't know anyway. I learnt that secrets kept you sick, when I remembered how many days I had been tormented by a 'phantom' problem.

Letting go of JT was actually not as hard as I feared it would be, when I really examined our lives together all I really saw were a variety of events, some good, some bad. I realised life was more than just getting out of it. JT and I had nothing really in common anymore. Sobriety being the precious commodity it was compensated for the loss of him. Becoming and staying visible was my full-time job these days. In my good moments I wished his trekking well, in the bad moments I threatened to go to Nepal to find him. I knew I couldn't and wouldn't, but the fierce girl in me enjoyed thinking I could if I wanted.

Moriatta Falls continues to welcome the waifs and strays who find themselves at their doors. The staff continue to be wonderful, non-judgemental and caring in the face of great difficulties at times.

All sorts of people find their way to rehab, addiction is the great leveller as they say. So everyone from Professors to travellers, to footballers and students can and do become sick through addiction.

Trouble and addiction go hand in hand, the progression of the disease is what alerts everyone to the fact that there are problems. Sometimes health is affected by the myriad of physical problems that can affect the body. Almost always relationships are affected. Some relationships make it and some like mine, Rita's and Brendon's sadly do not. Work is another area that can be seen to be affected, with mistakes, trouble and loss of jobs being common. Financial woes again are a common problem for people with addictions. Although alcohol and other drugs can be seen as relatively cheap commodities, the sheer volume of use and the trouble it brings often affects a person's ability to stay financially fit. The worst and most dangerous of problems perhaps is a person's mental health which deteriorates as long as the using continues.

The continuous assault on the brain and mind of humans can be catastrophic, if there are other mental health issues in dual diagnosis then the person is in deep trouble. There are almost always other mental health problems where addiction is concerned. Depression exists in almost every addict at the end of their using. It sometimes emerges when someone tries to get clean. Always having been present with the using masking or being the solution to the low feelings. It's not talked about, its denied, it's hidden. As all these things continue the world and addicts get sicker. Denial, after all, is the go-to attitude in all things about addiction, both in the addicts themselves but also more crazily in the public at large.

Moriatta Falls is despised and loved in equal measure. If no solution to the insanity is discovered then the facility and the people who work in it are vilified. If Recovery is found then they end up being loved. Mad? Insane? Of course, but oh my goodness how amazing when our 'best thinking' the thinking that brought us to our knees changes, to enable us to become the people we all really should be. The very best versions of ourselves.

> "You are asking yourself, as all of us must:
> 'Who am I?'…
> 'Where am I?'…
> 'Whence do I go?'
>
> The process of enlightenment is usually slow. But in the end, our seeking always brings a finding. These great mysteries are, after all, enshrined in complete simplicity. The willingness to grow is the essence of all spiritual development."

- Selected Writings by Bill W - The AA Way of Life

Resources

Alcoholics Anonymous – AA World Service – www.alcoholics-anonymous.org.uk

Sex Addicts Anonymous – www.saa-recovery.org

Cocaine Anonymous – www.cauk.org.uk

Gamblers Anonymous – www.gamblersanonymous.co.uk

Al-Anon – www.al-anonuk.org.uk and www.codependents.org

Overeaters Anonymous including Anorexia – www.oagb.org.uk

There are many more anonymous meetings available, contact with any of the above should open the doors to them all.

National Gambling Helpline – www.gamcare.org.uk

Samaritans – www.samaratins.org

Anti-Bullying Service – www.dabsonline.org and www.alisonfoxcounselling.co.uk

Pleasure Unwoven and Memo to Self DVDs – Kevin Macauley

Lou and Darcie Gannon – discussed with kind permission

Suicide Awareness discussed with permission from Fiona Penfold RMN

Angie Cullen RMN and FDAP therapist – Family therapist 07834 118781

Jacqui Newbold FDAP therapist - gave permission to discuss Aftercare Agreement

Addictive Thinking – Abraham J. Twerski, MD – Hazelden –

Bill Stevens – Interventionist – www.redchair.co.uk

Acknowledgements

Some grateful thanks to:

Libby Garnham for her on-going support and help in proofreading and editing and encouragement to keep going even when doubt comes calling.

Ben Wright for reminding me that 'my best thinking' is what it is all about.

Grateful thanks to Bill and Bob for saving my life and the lives of millions with their genius ideas of helping the suffering alcoholic.

The Fellowship for developing and growing and including all the new-fangled drugs and other crazy addictions.

To Steve Stephens for helping me see my truth.

Thanks to Kevin H, Duncan C, Bryan D, Paul W, Karen J and Julie Stokes, who have each gone above and beyond in helping me Change Perceptions one book at a time.

To Karen D for always being a true friend and available to help and assist in promoting my books.

For Mark Murphy for creating www.Seahab2020.com and in so doing inspiring me to continue the supersonic quest of changing perceptions.

Also by Sarina Wheatman

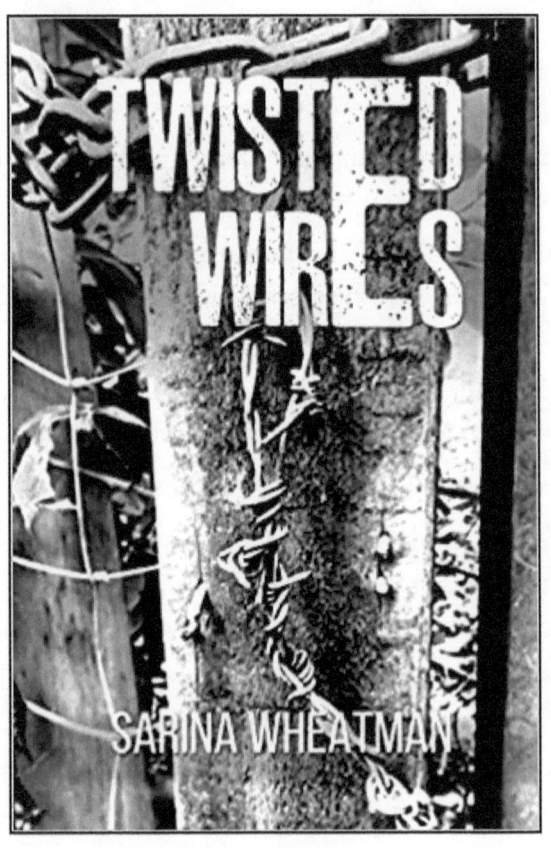

Untangling the world of addictions

Sarina Wheatman

*Available worldwide from Amazon
and all good bookstores*

**If you have enjoyed this book or
found it helpful…**
please leave an Amazon Review

Join me in my mission to
'Change Perceptions One Book at a Time'

**Contact Sarina Wheatman:
www.sarinawheatman.com**

---

www.mtp.agency

www.facebook.com/mtp.agency

@mtp_agency

www.ingramcontent.com/pod-product-compliance
Lightning Source LLC
LaVergne TN
LVHW091545060526
838200LV00036B/717